ALL-TIME GREATEST SOCCER STORIES FOR KIDS

10 INSPIRING JOURNEYS OF LEGENDARY PLAYERS, AMAZING GOALS, AND LIFE LESSONS TO TEACH, CAPTIVATE, AND MOTIVATE YOUNG READERS AND SOCCER FANS

CHRIS VILLANUEVA

© **Copyright 2024 by Chris Villanueva - All rights reserved.**

The content contained within this book may not be reproduced, duplicated, or transmitted without direct written permission from the author or the publisher. Under no circumstances will any blame or legal responsibility be held against the publisher or author for any damages, reparation, or monetary loss due to the information contained within this book, either directly or indirectly.

Legal Notice:

This book is copyright-protected. It is only for personal use. You cannot amend, distribute, sell, use, quote or paraphrase any part or the content within this book, without the consent of the author or publisher.

Disclaimer Notice:

Please note that the information contained within this document is for educational and entertainment purposes only. All effort has been executed to present accurate, up-to-date, and reliable, complete information. No warranties of any kind are declared or implied. Readers acknowledge that the author is not engaging in the rendering of legal, Financial, medical, or professional advice. The content within this book has been derived from various sources. Please consult a licensed professional before attempting any techniques outlined in this book. By reading this document, the reader agrees that under no circumstances is the author responsible for any losses, direct or indirect, which are incurred as a result of the use of the information contained within this document, including but not limited to errors, omissions, or inaccuracies

TABLE OF CONTENTS

Introduction	5
1. LIONEL MESSI: OVERCOMING HEALTH ISSUES	9
Off to Barcelona!	11
La Masia to First Team	13
Overcoming Setbacks	15
A Symbol Of Hope	16
2. CRISTIANO RONALDO: A LEGACY OF FIVE BALLON D'ORS	21
Historic Wins	23
Cementing His Status	25
Relentless Work Ethic and Self-Belief	26
Inspiration to Others	28
	30
3. PELÉ: FROM POVERTY TO GLOBAL FAME	33
Rising Through the Ranks	35
Worldwide Stardom	37
Money Troubles	39
Legacy	40
4. NEYMAR: EMBRACING INDIVIDUALITY AND SELF-EXPRESSION	43
Rising to Fame	46
Celebrating Individuality	47
Influence Beyond Soccer	49
Inspirational Figure	50
5. MEGAN RAPINOE: VOICE FOR EQUALITY AND CAPTAIN AMERICA	57
Voice for Fairness and Equality	59
Being A Team Leader	61
Personal Journey and Challenges	63
Inspirational Figure Worldwide	65

6. DIDIER DROGBA: UNITING A TORN COUNTRY	69
Didier's Ceasefire Plea	71
Influence Through Success	73
National Peace	74
Legacy of Leadership	76
	77
7. MIA HAMM: A GIRL'S STRUGGLE IN A BOY'S WORLD	79
Supportive Family Environment	81
Development as a National Player	82
Leadership and Team Success	84
8. HOMARE SAWA - PERSEVERANCE AND LEADERSHIP	89
At Home and Across the World	91
World Cup Triumph	92
A Role Model for Japan and Beyond	94
Overcoming Setbacks and Continuing to Win	96
9. SADIO MANE: A STAR WITH A BIG HEART	101
Climbing the Ranks	103
Success at Liverpool	105
Giving Back	107
Inspirational Figure	109
10. DIEGO MARADONA: HANDLING MISTAKES AND CONTROVERSY	113
Reaction and Controversy	115
Maradona's Two-Sided Legacy	117
Staying Focused	119
Lasting Impact on Soccer	120
Conclusion	123
References	127

INTRODUCTION

Alright, kids and parents, lace up your cleats and get ready for an incredible journey into the heart of soccer! Picture this: the stadium lights are blazing, the crowd's cheers are deafening, and the tension on the field is electric. It's the final match of the World Cup. The score is tied, and one player steps forward to take the deciding penalty kick. The entire world seems to hold its breath. Will they make history? Will they become the hero their team desperately needs?

That heart-stopping moment is just a snapshot of what soccer is all about. But here's the secret: the real magic isn't just in the game —it's in the stories behind the players who make those moments special. These are stories of relentless hard work, determination, and unshakeable dreams. They're stories of overcoming challenges, battling doubts, and rising to the top, no matter how tough the journey.

This book isn't your usual soccer guide filled with stats and game recaps. It's a collection of inspiring tales from the lives of ten extraordinary soccer stars who chased their dreams and made them a reality. Each chapter is a deep dive into the life of one player, exploring their unique journey—their triumphs, setbacks, and the grit that got them through. These aren't just sports stories; they're life lessons, told through the lens of the world's most popular game.

What makes this book extra special is its diversity. Soccer is the world's game, played in every corner by people of all genders, ethnicities, and backgrounds. And the players featured here reflect that. From fields in bustling cities to dusty pitches in small villages, their stories show how soccer unites us all and prove that talent, determination, and hard work know no borders.

For young readers aged 8 to 13, this book is your ticket to discovering what it takes to be a champion—not just in sports, but in life. Whether you're a die-hard soccer fan or someone looking for a bit of inspiration, you'll find something to encourage you on these pages. And this is for parents too. These stories are written to be fun and engaging, full of lessons about resilience, teamwork, and dreaming big. Who knows? Parents might find themselves turning pages long after the kids have gone to bed!

So, what can you expect as we embark on this adventure? You'll meet players who started with nothing but a ball and a dream. You'll follow their struggles, celebrate their wins, and see how they became role models for millions. Through their stories, you'll learn that failure isn't the end—it's just the beginning of a new chance to grow. You'll discover that hard work beats talent when talent doesn't work hard. And you'll see that no matter where you come from, the sky's the limit when you believe in yourself.

Get ready to step into the shoes of these soccer legends. Feel the sweat on their brows, the weight of their dreams, and the fire in their hearts. By the end of this book, you won't just know more about soccer; you'll feel inspired to tackle your own challenges with the same passion and perseverance.

So grab your favorite snack, get comfy, and let's kick off this incredible journey together. Let's discover what it really means to be a champion—on the field and in life.

Lionel Messi

CHAPTER ONE
LIONEL MESSI: OVERCOMING HEALTH ISSUES

"You have to fight to reach your dream. You have to sacrifice and work hard for it"

LIONEL MESSI

Let's kick off our group of amazing stories with one of the greatest soccer plays of all time, Lionel Messi. You may have heard of Lionel Messi; if not, that's okay. He's one of the biggest soccer superstars of our lifetimes and considered one of the best to ever play the game. However, before becoming that soccer superstar we know, he faced a very tough challenge growing up. Let's rewind to the small town of Rosario, Argentina, where Lionel spent his early years. Imagine yourself as young Lionel, a kid just like you with a big dream but an impossible hurdle.

When Lionel Messi was just a young kid, his parents saw something strange. Lionel was growing less than the other kids his age. When Lionel was just ten years old, the doctors told him that he had a problem called growth hormone deficiency. This meant his body didn't have the right hormones he needed to grow properly. Imagine being told you might never grow big enough to compete in the sport you love. That was Lionel and his family. It also wasn't just about soccer; it was about his health and well-being.

Of course, his family was really worried. His parents, Jorge and Celia, were heartbroken. They knew their son had so much talent for soccer, but they knew he would need treatment for his dreams to come true. Treatment required expensive daily injections, something that was way beyond what their family could afford. The emotional toll was heavy, not just on Lionel, who felt different from his friends, but on his entire family, who were doing everything they could to support him.

Despite the challenges, Lionel's love for soccer was stronger than ever. He kept playing with his friends and in local clubs, even though he was much smaller than the other kids. The local soccer clubs in Rosario saw his potential and tried to help as much as they could. They provided him with opportunities to play and develop his skills, but there was always a limit because of his size. The cost of treatment was a constant barrier. Still, the endless support meant a lot to young Lionel and his family, showing them they weren't alone in their struggle.

For Lionel, the hardest part wasn't just the physical part of his condition but the emotional and social challenges. He often felt like an outsider because of his size. Playing soccer with other kids, he was teased and doubted. People would tell him he was too small to make it in soccer. But if there's one thing you should know about Lionel Messi, it is that he has the heart of a lion. He didn't let those words get to him. Instead, he used them as fuel to prove everyone wrong. Every time he stepped onto the field, he played with a powerful determination, turning his size into an advantage with his speed and agility.

Lionel Messi's childhood years were filled with uncertainty and struggle, but they were also defined by incredible resilience and support from his family and community. His story is a powerful reminder that no matter what challenges you face, you can overcome them with hard work and support from your community.

OFF TO BARCELONA!

When Lionel Messi was just 13 years old, he and his family made a huge decision that would change their lives forever. They packed their bags and moved from Rosario, Argentina, to Barcelona, Spain. It's very tough leaving everything you know behind—your friends, school, your favorite places—and going to a different country where everything is different. But for Messi, they needed to make this move because FC Barcelona had offered him a chance to join their youth academy, La Masia. FC Barcelona is one of the biggest soccer clubs in the world. They also promised to cover the cost of his medical treatments. It was a dream come true, but it came with its challenges.

The language barrier was challenging. Messi spoke Spanish, but the Catalan dialect spoken in Barcelona was new to him. Understanding coaches, making friends, and even simple things like ordering food became complicated. But Messi and his family were determined. They knew this was a once-in-a-lifetime opportunity, so they embraced the change and worked hard to adapt to their new country.

The move to Spain was also hard for his family financially. While FC Barcelona covered the cost of his medical treatments, there were still plenty of other expenses to worry about, such as renting an apartment, buying groceries, and other day-to-day expenses that added up quickly. Messi's father, Jorge, had to work multiple jobs to make ends meet. His mother, Celia, had to manage the house and support Lionel. The whole family made sacrifices, but it was worth it to them. They believed in Lionel's talent and were committed to helping him achieve his dreams.

Even though they faced financial and cultural hurdles, Messi found a lot of support at FC Barcelona. The club didn't just see him as another player; they saw him as part of their family. Coaches and staff members went out of their way to make him feel welcome. They helped him adjust to his new life on and off the field. Mentors at La Masia provided guidance, teaching him not just about soccer but also about life. They offered tips on handling pressure, staying focused, and pushing forward, no matter what.

The youth academy, La Masia, became a second home to Messi. He met other young players who also moved far from home and quickly became friends. These friendships helped Messi feel less alone and more connected to his new environment. The intense training sessions and competition pushed him to work hard and improve every day. Coaches saw his potential and worked hard to help him develop his skills. They encouraged him to use his small stature to his advantage, focusing on speed, agility, and ball control.

Through all of this, Messi's family remained his rock. They attended every match, cheered him on, and provided the emotional support he needed to stay motivated. Their belief in Messi gave him the strength to keep going, even when things got tough. The sacrifices they made were immense, but they knew it was all worth it when they saw Lionel play. Their unwavering support is a testament to the power of family in overcoming challenges.

Messi's move to Barcelona was a defining moment in his life. It was a time of immense change, filled with challenges but also opportunities. It tested his resilience, his adaptability, and his determination. Despite the struggles, Messi thrived. He had the support of his family, the mentorship of his coaches, and the friendship of his teammates. All of this created a foundation that would help him become the soccer legend we know today.

LA MASIA TO FIRST TEAM

When Messi joined FC Barcelona's youth academy, La Masia, it was like stepping into a soccer wonderland. La Masia is known for turning talented kids into soccer superstars, and Messi was about to find out why. The training there was intense and designed to push players to their limits. Messi would spend hours perfecting his dribbling, shooting, and passing. Coaches emphasized being skillful, smart, and very fit. Every day was a new challenge and a time to shine for Messi. His skill development was incredible. He had this cool ability to control the ball as if it were glued to his feet. His quickness and agility were off the charts, making him a nightmare for defenders.

From the start, Messi's talent was obvious. Coaches and peers quickly noticed his standout performances. There were so many stories of him dribbling past the entire team during practice matches. One time, during a game against much older kids, Messi weaved through five defenders and scored a spectacular goal. His teammates were amazed, and the coaches knew they had someone special on their hands. They began to pay extra attention to him and offer more personal training and encouragement. The talk around La Masia was that this small kid from Argentina was destined for greatness. His peers, though doubted him at first because of his size, soon realized that Messi was a star in the making.

But it wasn't all smooth sailing. Messi had to overcome several obstacles, including his small body and fierce competition. La

Masia was filled with talented players, all going for a spot on the first team. Messi's small stature was often a disadvantage in physical battles. There were times when he was pushed around and knocked off the ball. However, Messi turned these challenges into opportunities. He focused on what he was great at—speed, agility, and ball control. He worked hard to improve his balance and strength so that he could hold his own against bigger opponents. The competition was fierce, but Messi's determination was fiercer. He spent extra hours practicing, often staying long after his teammates had left the field.

Messi's hard work and talent were eventually noticed. His big break came when he was just 16 years old. FC Barcelona's first team coach, Frank Rijkaard, had heard about the young prodigy and decided to give him a chance. First team is a soccer club's best team. Imagine the excitement and nerves of a 16-year-old stepping onto the field with some of the biggest names in soccer. Messi made his debut in a friendly match against Porto, a Portuguese soccer club. It was a huge moment, not just for Messi but for everyone who had supported him. He played with the same confidence and flair he had shown in La Masia. It was clear that he was ready for the big stage.

Messi's first team debut was more than just a game; it was a statement. It marked the beginning of a new chapter in his career. Now, the world was going to see Lionel Messi's potential. Messi continued to work hard, knowing that this was just the start. He faced new challenges, but each one only made him stronger. His journey through the ranks of La Masia to the first team was a testament to his resilience, talent, and unyielding determination. It showed that even the most daunting obstacles could be overcome with hard work and perseverance.

Messi's rapid rise through the ranks of La Masia is a powerful reminder that greatness isn't handed to you; it's earned through hard work, dedication, and a relentless pursuit of excellence.

OVERCOMING SETBACKS

Lionel Messi was not immune to setbacks. He also had to deal with some pretty serious injuries. One of the most significant injuries in Messi's career happened in 2006 when he fractured the metatarsal bone in his left foot. Ouch, right? It wasn't just a minor scratch; it was a serious injury that kept him off the field for three months. For someone who lives and breathes soccer, this was hard. It wasn't just about the physical pain; the emotional pain of not being able to play was intense. He had to watch his team play without him. But Messi didn't let this setback define him.

The recovery wasn't easy. It required a lot of hard work, dedication, and patience. Messi focused on his recovery exercises with the same intensity he brought to the soccer field. Physical therapy sessions, strength training, and endless hours of practice to regain his form and fitness became his new routine. There were days when progress seemed so slow, but Messi's heart never wavered. He knew that to get back to his best, he had to put in the effort, no matter how tough it got. It's like when you're learning a new skill, and it feels like your progress is slow. Slowly but surely, Messi made his comeback, stronger and more determined than ever.

Handling criticism was another challenge Messi faced. Despite his undeniable talent, there were always critics who questioned his style of play or compared him harshly to other players. Some said he relied too much on his left foot, while others doubted his ability to perform in important games. Criticism can be tough to handle, especially when giving your all. Instead of letting negative comments get him down, he used them as motivation to improve.

He worked on his weaknesses, improved his skills, and proved his doubters wrong game after game. It's like when someone tells you that you can't do something, and you work extra hard to show them that you can.

These setbacks and criticisms didn't just challenge Messi; they also played a crucial role in his personal growth. Each injury and each piece of criticism was a learning experience. They taught him to be strong, stay focused, and the value of hard work. Overcoming these challenges made him a better player and a stronger person. It's like leveling up in a game; each challenge you overcome makes you better prepared for the next one. Messi's journey is a testament to how setbacks can be turned into stepping stones for success.

Messi learned to stay calm under pressure, to keep pushing forward even when things seemed bleak, and to always believe in himself. These lessons are valuable not just in soccer but in any aspect of life. Whether it's dealing with a difficult school project, facing a personal challenge, or pursuing a dream, Messi's story shows that with determination and hard work, you can overcome anything. So, next time you face a setback, remember Lionel Messi and keep pushing forward.

A SYMBOL OF HOPE

Lionel Messi's story is more than just one of athletic skills; it's a symbol of hope and determination for everyone around the world. Facing tough challenges could have easily derailed his dreams, yet instead, he turned it into the fuel that powered his journey. When people hear Messi's name, they don't just think of his dazzling dribbles and breathtaking goals. They think of a person who refused to let obstacles define him. It's as if he's telling every kid out there, "Hey, if I can do it, so can you."

Over the years, he has received many awards and honors that recognize not just his talent but his perseverance. Messi's trophy cabinet is overflowing from winning multiple Ballon d'Or awards —an award given to the best player in the world—to receiving the Golden Foot award. Each award is a testament to his hard work and resilience. These celebrations of his journey add to his legacy, showing that he's not just a player but a symbol of what can be done through hard work. Every time Messi steps up to accept an award, it's a reminder to everyone watching that dreams are within reach if you're willing to fight for them.

Reflecting on his journey, Messi often speaks about the importance of resilience. He's shared in interviews that his setbacks and challenges have shaped him into the person he is today. Messi talks about how every injury, every criticism, and every obstacle taught him valuable lessons. He emphasizes that resilience isn't just about bouncing back but about growing stronger with each fall. For Messi, the journey to the top wasn't a straight line. It was filled with twists and turns, each teaching him the value of not giving up. His reflections serve as a powerful message to young readers: setbacks are not the end but the beginning of a new chapter.

The impact of Messi's story extends far beyond the soccer field. His journey has touched hearts around the world, inspiring not just fans but people from all walks of life. Messi uses his platform to give back to the community by engaging in charity. Through his foundation, he supports access to education and healthcare for less fortunate children, ensuring they have opportunities to thrive. Messi's advocacy for medical treatment access, especially for growth hormone deficiency, has brought attention to health disparities. He is helping kids overcome the same challenges he experienced as a young kid.

No dream is too big, and no challenge is too great. Messi's life is a testament to the idea that you can overcome any obstacle with hard work, dedication, and a bit of support. It's about turning challenges into opportunities and never giving up, no matter how tough things get. So, whenever you're faced with a hurdle, think of Lionel Messi. Remember his story, his resilience, and his determination. Let it inspire you to keep pushing forward, to chase your dreams, and to become your own hero. Just like Messi, you have the power to achieve greatness, both on and off the field.

Activity: Finding Your Messi Moment

Lionel Messi's story is one of never giving up, humility, and staying true to yourself, even in the face of incredible challenges. Think about a time when you faced an obstacle that seemed impossible to overcome. Maybe it was a tough class at school, learning a new skill, or dealing with something personal. How did you approach it? Did you push through, even when it felt overwhelming? How did it feel to keep going, and what did you learn from the experience?

Write about this moment in your journal. Reflect on how you can channel Messi's resilience the next time you face a challenge. What steps can you take to stay focused, believe in yourself, and work toward your goals, no matter how big they seem?

Messi's journey reminds us that success doesn't come easy—it takes dedication, patience, and staying grounded. Whether it's dealing with setbacks or staying humble in moments of victory, there's so much to learn from the way Messi carries himself on and off the field. As you move forward, think about how you can embody that same spirit of determination and kindness in your own life, both on and off the field.

Ronaldo

CHAPTER TWO
CRISTIANO RONALDO: A LEGACY OF FIVE BALLON D'ORS

"Talent without working hard is nothing"

CRISTIANO RONALDO

Imagine yourself on a tiny island, surrounded by the vast Ocean, where the waves crash against rocky cliffs and the air is filled with the scent of saltwater. This is Madeira, Portugal—the birthplace of Cristiano Ronaldo. Imagine young Cristiano running barefoot through the narrow streets, a soccer ball never far from his feet.

Growing up in Madeira wasn't easy for Cristiano. His family lived in a small, modest home, and money was always tight. His father, José Dinis Aveiro, worked as a gardener and a part-time kit man at a local soccer club. At the same time, his mother, Maria Dolores, often had to take on extra jobs to help make ends meet. Despite these economic challenges, the Aveiro family was close-knit and supportive. They might not have had much, but they had each other. And they had soccer. From a young age, Ronaldo showed an incredible passion for the game. It was more than just a pastime for him; it was a way of life.

Even as a young boy, Ronaldo's talent on the soccer field was undeniable. He had a natural gift for the game, with an uncanny ability to control the ball and a relentless drive to score goals. His family recognized this talent and did everything they could to nurture it. Despite his long hours at work, his father would take Ronaldo to practice and matches, always cheering him on from the sidelines. His mother, too, was his biggest fan, encouraging him to pursue his dreams no matter the obstacles. They believed in him, and that belief became key to his success.

Ronaldo's journey took a big turn when he moved to Lisbon to join Sporting CP's academy. Imagine leaving your home at just 12 years old and moving to a big city where you know no one, all in the pursuit of a dream. That's what Ronaldo did. It was a huge sacrifice, not just for him but for his entire family. In Lisbon, Ronaldo faced new challenges. He had to adapt to a new environment, away from the comfort of his family. The training was extreme, and the competition was intense. But Ronaldo thrived. He saw every challenge as an opportunity to prove himself. His commitment was unwavering, and his drive was unmatched.

Even from a young age, Ronaldo's work ethic was extraordinary. He wasn't just talented; he was relentlessly pursuing to be a superstar. While other kids were out playing or watching TV, Ronaldo was training. He would spend hours practicing dribbling, shooting, and passing, often staying on the field after his teammates had gone home. He was known for his intense work ethic, pushing himself to the limit every single day. It wasn't just about natural talent; it was about hard work, dedication, and a burning desire to be the best. Ronaldo's commitment to his training set the foundation for his future success.

Ronaldo's story is a powerful reminder that talent alone isn't enough. The combination of talent, hard work, and an unyielding commitment to your goals leads to true greatness. His early life in Madeira, the support of his family, and his relentless work ethic from a young age all played a crucial role in shaping him into the soccer legend he is today.

HISTORIC WINS

All that hard work led Cristiano Ronald to become one of the best players in the world. In 2008, he achieved something incredible - he won his first Ballon d'Or. The Ballon d'Or is like the Oscars for soccer players, awarded to the best player in the world each year. Ronaldo's win in 2008 was massive. Playing for Manchester United at the time, he had an incredible season, scoring 42 goals and helping his team win the Premier League and the UEFA Champions League. The moment he was handed the golden trophy, it was a dream come true for Ronaldo and everyone who had supported him. This win was a statement. It announced to the soccer world that Cristiano Ronaldo had arrived and was here to stay. From that moment on, his career took on a new level.

Ronaldo didn't stop there. After his first Ballon d'Or, he continued pushing himself, aiming to be the best ever year. He won another Ballon d'Or in 2013, this time while playing for Real Madrid. That season, he scored a jaw-dropping 55 goals in just 55 games. The sheer consistency and brilliance of his performances were undeniable. Then, in 2014, he did it again, winning his third Ballon d'Or. This time, he led Real Madrid to their long-awaited 10th Champions League title. This accomplishment earned him even more respect and admiration. It was like watching a superhero in action; every game was another chapter in an epic story.

In 2016, Ronaldo added another Ballon d'Or to his collection. That year was particularly special because it wasn't just about club success but an entire country's success. Ronaldo also led Portugal to victory in the UEFA European Championship. This win was historic for Portugal, as it was their first major international trophy. Ronaldo's joy and tears of happiness after the final whistle were seen by millions. It was a moment that showed his skill and immense passion for the game and his country. Finally, in 2017, Ronaldo won his fifth Ballon d'Or, again proving his unusual talent and dedication. That year, he led Real Madrid to another Champions League title and was the tournament's top scorer. Ronaldo solidified his status as one of the greatest players ever graced the soccer field with each trophy.

Each year, Ronaldo faced fierce competition for the Ballon d'Or. One of his biggest competitors was Lionel Messi. The rivalry between Ronaldo and Messi is legendary, often described as one of the greatest in sports history. Every year, fans and pundits would debate who was better, and the Ballon d'Or ceremonies often came down to these two giants. Other top players like Neymar and Andrés Iniesta also vied for the coveted trophy, making each win even more significant. Ronaldo thrived under this pressure. Competing against the best brought out the best in him. It was like a never-ending game of one-upmanship, pushing Ronaldo to new heights each season.

Winning the Ballon d'Or once is a remarkable achievement, but winning it five times is extraordinary. For Ronaldo, these wins were a testament to his relentless hard work, his determination, and his thirst for success. Each award marked another year of excellence and another chapter in his incredible career. These wins also set new standards of excellence, inspiring countless young players to dream big and work hard. Ronaldo's Ballon d'Or victories were not just personal triumphs; they were moments that captured the imagination of soccer fans everywhere, reminding us all why we love the beautiful game.

CEMENTING HIS STATUS

Winning multiple Ballon d'Or awards gave Ronaldo the status of one of the greatest footballers of all time. They were like golden stamps of approval, marking his place in soccer history. Every award elevated his career, impacting decisions on where to play next and what contracts to sign. Soccer clubs around the world knew that signing Ronaldo wasn't just about getting a player; it was about getting a global icon. His value soared, and he became one of the highest-paid athletes in the world.

Ronaldo's success on the field translated into massive business success. Think about it—everyone wants a piece of you when you win the Ballon d'Or. Brands lined up to have Ronaldo support their products. Everyone wanted Ronaldo to be the face of their campaigns, from sportswear giants like Nike to luxury brands like TAG Heuer. His image was everywhere, from billboards to TV commercials, and his social media following exploded. His brand became as valuable as his soccer skills, bringing millions through endorsements and sponsorships. This commercial success made him a household name, even among people who didn't follow soccer.

Ronaldo's impact was also felt on every team he played for. When he joined Manchester United, he brought a level of skill and flair that transformed the team. His presence on the field was electrifying, and his ability to score goals from unbelievable positions lifted the entire squad. At Real Madrid, he took things to another level. His goalscoring record was phenomenal, and he played a crucial role in helping the team win multiple Champions League titles. His success elevated the team's status, making them the team to beat in Europe. Moving to Juventus, he brought the same level of excellence, helping them dominate the Italian league. Ronaldo's success was shared by every team he played for, elevating them to new heights.

Globally, Ronaldo's praise and respect are incredible. Kids from small villages around the world know who Ronaldo is. That's the level of global fame he has achieved. His peers respect him not just for his skills but for his dedication and work ethic. Fans around the world love him, filling stadiums just to catch a glance of him in action. His impact extends beyond soccer, making him a role model for aspiring athletes in all sports. Ronaldo's story of rising from humble beginnings to global stardom is a beacon of hope and inspiration. His awards and success have made him a symbol of what can be achieved with hard work and determination, and his global recognition is a testament to the extent of his influence.

RELENTLESS WORK ETHIC AND SELF-BELIEF

Let's talk about what makes Cristiano Ronaldo an incredible player. One of the secrets behind his success is his relentless training program. Even before the sun is up, Ronaldo starts the day with a vigorous workout. His dedication to training is legendary. He doesn't just show up to practice; he dominates it. Every session is meticulously planned to push him to work hard. He works on his speed, agility, and endurance, making sure that he's always in peak condition. It's like having a superhero training routine but without the cape. Ronaldo's ability to perform at high levels is a result of this intense and disciplined approach to training.

But it's not just about the workouts. Ronaldo's entire day is a masterclass in fitness and self-discipline. He follows a strict diet that fuels his body for optimal performance. Imagine eating six small meals a day, packed with lean meat, whole grains, and plenty of vegetables. That's Ronaldo's diet in a nutshell. He avoids sugary snacks and junk food, focusing on foods that give him energy. He drinks plenty of water to stay hydrated and keep his muscles functioning at their best. This commitment to physical fitness sets him apart from many of his peers. It's not just about playing soccer but about living a lifestyle supporting his goals. Ronaldo's routine includes not just about his body but also his mind. He works on keeping his mind strong and imagining his games ahead of time.

Ronaldo's self-belief is a crucial factor in his success. Imagine standing in a stadium with thousands of fans, all eyes on you, waiting for you to take a penalty kick. The pressure is immense, but Ronaldo thrives under it. His strong mind allows him to stay calm and focused, even in the most high-stakes situations. He believes in his abilities and that confidence is contagious. It's not arrogance; it's a deep-seated belief in his preparation and skills. This mental toughness didn't come overnight. It's something he's developed over years of facing challenges and overcoming obstacles. Ronaldo's self-belief fuels his determination, pushing him towards greatness, no matter the chances.

One of the coolest things about Ronaldo is his philosophy of continuous improvement. You'd think that after winning numerous awards and breaking countless records, he might be satisfied. But Ronaldo is never comfortable with past accomplishments. He's always looking for ways to get better. Whether improving his technique and fitness or studying his opponents, Ronaldo constantly seeks ways to elevate his game. This relentless pursuit of perfection keeps him at the top of his sport. He understands that there's always room for growth and embraces the challenge of becoming better every day. Ronaldo's dedication to continuous improvement is a powerful reminder that success is a journey, not a destination.

Ronaldo's intense training and unwavering self-belief are not just about soccer; they're life lessons. They teach us the importance of hard work, discipline, and the power of believing in ourselves. Whether you aim to be a soccer star or excel in any other area of life, Ronaldo's approach can inspire you to push your limits and strive for greatness. So next time you face a challenge, remember Ronaldo's dedication and let it motivate you to keep going, to keep improving, and to never settle for anything less than your best.

INSPIRATION TO OTHERS

As we wrap up this story, let's notice that Cristiano Ronaldo isn't just a soccer superstar; he's a symbol of inspiration for kids around the world. His consistent greatness on the field, his flashy skills, and his relentless drive—all of these things make him a hero to aspiring athletes everywhere. Kids look up to him not just because he wins trophies but because he shows them what's possible with hard work and determination. They see a player who never settles, who always pushes himself to be better, and they think, "If Ronaldo can do it, maybe I can too."

But Ronaldo's influence doesn't stop at being a role model from afar. He actively mentors young players, offering advice and encouragement whenever he can. Whether it's a quick chat after a game or a more formal mentoring session, Ronaldo takes the time to share his knowledge and experience. He talks about the importance of hard work, staying focused, and never giving up, no matter how tough things get. For a young player, getting advice from Ronaldo is like getting tips from a superhero. It's incredibly motivating and helps them believe in their own potential. Ronaldo's willingness to give back to the next generation of players shows how much he cares about the sport and its future.

Public speaking is another way Ronaldo inspires others. He's not just a player who lets his feet do the talking; he's also a powerful speaker. Ronaldo often participates in events where he talks about his life, career, and the lessons he's learned. He shares stories of his early struggles, his sacrifices, and the hard work that got him to where he is today. These talks are filled with wisdom and inspiration, encouraging everyone to persevere and chase their dreams. Hearing Ronaldo speak about his journey makes the idea of achieving greatness seem more attainable. It's like getting a pep talk from someone who's been through it all and come out on top.

Ronaldo's legacy is something that will last long after he hangs up his boots. His dedication to the sport, his incredible achievements, and his willingness to inspire and mentor others all contribute to a lasting impact. Young players will continue to look up to him, drawing inspiration from his career and his words. Coaches will use Ronaldo's story to motivate their teams, teaching them the values of hard work and perseverance. Even fans who don't play soccer can find lessons in Ronaldo's story, applying his determination and work ethic to their own lives. Ronaldo's legacy isn't just about the goals he scored or the trophies he won; it's about the lives he touched and the inspiration he provided to countless people around the world.

Ronaldo's journey from a young boy in Madeira to a global soccer icon is a testament to what can be achieved with hard work, dedication, and a bit of inspiration. His consistent excellence, willingness to mentor young players, powerful public speaking, and lasting legacy all combine to make him one of the most influential athletes of all time. As we move to the next chapter, we'll explore Neymar, another soccer legend who has inspired millions with her incredible journey and dedication to the sport.

Activity: Working Hard Like Cristiano Ronaldo

Cristiano Ronaldo is known for his amazing talent, but his real superpower is how hard he works to be the best. Think about a time when you worked really hard for something you wanted. Maybe it was practicing a sport, studying for a test, or learning something new. How did it feel to put in that effort? Were you proud of what you achieved?

Write about this in your journal. Think about how you can keep working hard, even when things get tough. What can you do to stay focused on your goals? How can you remind yourself that hard work pays off, just like it does for Ronaldo?

Ronaldo's story shows us that talent is only part of the journey—it's dedication and effort that take you to the top. Whether you're chasing a big dream or just trying to get better at something, his example reminds us that we can achieve amazing things if we give it our all. How can you use Ronaldo's determination to reach your goals and become your best self?

Pelé

CHAPTER THREE
PELÉ: FROM POVERTY TO GLOBAL FAME

"Success is no accident. It is hard work, perseverance, learning, studying, sacrifice and most of all, love of what you are doing or learning to do."

PELÉ

Imagine a dusty street in a small Brazilian neighborhood; kids are running around barefoot, kicking what looks like a ball but is really just a bunch of socks wrapped up together. The sun is shining bright, and the air is filled with the sound of laughter as everyone chases that makeshift ball with dreams of glory in their hearts. Among these kids is a boy named Edson Arantes do Nascimento, but you probably know him better by his nickname, Pelé.

Pelé's early life was very humble. Born in Três Corações, a poor neighborhood in Brazil, Pelé grew up in a world where luxury was just a dream. His family lived in a small, cramped house that wasn't very comfortable. His father, Dondinho, was a former soccer player who never made it big, and his mother, Celeste, worked hard to make ends meet. Money was always limited, and there were days when even eating a decent meal was a luxury. But despite the money troubles and humble living conditions, one thing brought joy to Pelé's life—soccer.

Pelé was amazed by the game from the moment he could walk. He had no money for a soccer ball, so he made it work with whatever he could find—old socks stuffed with rags or grapefruits. It didn't matter to him because what mattered was the joy of playing, the excitement of kicking something around and imagining himself as a soccer star. Pelé and his friends would spend hours playing on the streets, creating goalposts with sticks and stones. They would treat every game like it was a mini World Cup. Even though it was simple, it was during these games that Pelé's passion for soccer truly began to blossom.

Pelé's father, Dondinho, played a huge role in growing Pelé's talent. Even though Dondinho's soccer career never took off, he saw the spark and potential in his son. He would spend hours teaching Pelé the basics of the game. They practiced dribbling, shooting, and passing in their small backyard. Dondinho's teaching was valuable, teaching Pelé the right skills and growing his love for the game and belief in himself. Dondinho used to tell him, "You have a gift, my son. Use it well." Those words stuck with Pelé and became a driving force in his life.

As Pelé got even better, it was obvious that he was no ordinary kid playing soccer on the streets! His talent was obvious, and it wasn't long before he caught the eye of some coaches. At 11 years old, he joined a local youth team called Bauru Athletic Club. This was a big step for young Pelé. Playing for a real team meant better training and actual games against other teams. It was here that Pelé started to get noticed for his skills. He had a natural gift for dribbling, a powerful shot, and an ability to read the game.

Coaches and teammates were amazed at how such a small kid could be so talented.

Pelé's journey with Bauru Athletic Club was filled with great moments. He would often outshine players much older and bigger than him! His performances on the field were spectacular, and word of his talent began to spread. People started coming to watch the matches to see this young sensation in action. It wasn't just his skills that impressed everyone; it was his passion, hard work, and never-give-up attitude. Pelé played every match as if it were the World Cup final, always giving his best effort on the field.

Even with his growing popularity, Pelé remained humble and focused. He knew talent alone wasn't enough; hard work and focus were just as important. He kept training tirelessly, always looking for ways to improve. His family gave him so much support. They may not have had much money, but they were rich in love and encouragement. Every time Pelé stepped onto the field, he carried with him the dreams and hopes of his family and his community.

Pelé's early life is a testament to the power of passion, hard work, and support. From playing with fake soccer balls on the streets to joining a local youth team, every step of his journey was fueled by his love for soccer and his family's unwavering belief. His story is a reminder that no matter where you start, with determination and support, you can achieve greatness.

RISING THROUGH THE RANKS

Pelé's journey from local youth teams to the bright lights of pro soccer began with a breakthrough. While playing for Bauru Athletic Club, his talent caught the eye of a former Brazilian national team player, Waldemar de Brito. Waldemar was so impressed that he convinced Pelé's family to let him take the young star to practice with Santos FC, one of Brazil's top clubs. Imagine packing your bags as a teenager and heading to a big city, all for a shot at your dreams. Pelé did just that, and it was a decision that would change his life forever.

Once at Santos FC, Pelé wasted no time making an impression. His skills and mindset on the field impressed both the coaches and players. Despite being just 15 years old, he played with the confidence of someone much older. Pelé rose quickly! Within months of joining Santos, Pelé was promoted to the senior squad.

Of course, not everyone was convinced. Some people wondered whether such a young and small player could handle the physical demands of professional soccer. They questioned whether Pelé could maintain his performance against tougher, more experienced players. But Pelé kept on proving people wrong. He faced these doubts head-on, letting his feet do the talking. He played with fire and determination every time he stepped onto the field. His agility and speed allowed him to weave through defenses, while his powerful shots often left goalkeepers helpless. By the end of his first season, even the harshest critics had to admit that Pelé was the real deal.

One of the biggest days ever for Pelé and his family was when Santos FC offered him a professional contract. It wasn't just a piece of paper; it was a lifeline for his family. The money he earned from his contract lifted his family out of poverty, providing them with a level of comfort they had never known. For Pelé, signing that contract was a huge moment. He was being rewarded for his hard work and talent. He knew that his success on the field was changing his family's life for the better. This new stability allowed his parents to focus on supporting him without any worry about money. This was such an emotional feeling for Pelé.

Pelé immediately had a strong impact on his team. His presence on the field was electrifying, and his performances quickly drew attention from fans and media. He wasn't just a player; he was a sensation. Crowds flocked to watch him play, amazed by his skill and flair. His ability to score goals against tough defenses earned him a reputation as one of soccer's most exciting young talents. Santos FC, too, benefited widely from Pelé's rise. The team's performance improved significantly, and they started winning more matches, mostly thanks to their new star player. Pelé's success brought a wave of excitement and optimism to the club, as well as increased attention from sponsors and media.

Overcoming skepticism and proving his worth at such a young age was no small feat. Pelé's journey through the ranks of Santos FC demonstrated not just his incredible talent but also his resilience and determination. He faced every challenge head-on, using every doubt and criticism as motivation to push harder and achieve more. His story is an example of the power of resilience and determination in the face of adversity.

WORLDWIDE STARDOM

At just 17 years old, Pelé was on the world's biggest stage: the 1958 World Cup in Sweden. Imagine being a teenager, and suddenly, everyone around the globe is watching you. That's a lot of pressure, right? But Pelé didn't just rise to the occasion; he soared! During the quarterfinals against Wales, he scored the only goal of the match, leading Brazil to victory. But it was the final against Sweden that truly cemented his legend. In that match, Pelé scored twice, helping Brazil secure a 5-2 win. His first goal was beautiful —a flick over a defender's head followed by a volley into the net. With this dazzling move, Pelé became the youngest player to score in a World Cup final, a record that still stands. His breakout performance didn't just win Brazil the World Cup; it introduced the world to a new soccer sensation.

Pelé didn't stop there. He continued to dominate soccer around the world, leading Brazil to World Cup victories in 1962 and 1970. In the 1962 World Cup held in Chile, Pelé was once again expected to lead Brazil to glory. Unfortunately, an injury in the second match sidelined him for most of the tournament. But even from the sidelines, his presence was felt. His teammates were inspired to step up, and Brazil won the tournament. Fast forward to the 1970 World Cup in Mexico, and Pelé was back, stronger and more determined than ever. This time, he wasn't just a young player; he was a leader. He scored four goals during the tournament, including one in the final against Italy, where Brazil won 4-1. His leadership on and off the field was instrumental in Brazil's victory, and he was named the best player of the tournament.

Pelé's success on the international stage did wonders for Brazilian soccer. Before Pelé, Brazil was known for its passion for the game, but it wasn't considered a soccer powerhouse. Pelé changed all that! His incredible performances attracted global attention, putting Brazilian soccer on the map. The world was fascinated by Brazil's unique style of play—fast, skillful, and full of flair. Pelé's success inspired a generation of young Brazilian players to dream big, knowing that they, too, could achieve greatness. It wasn't just about winning trophies but changing what people thought of Brazilian soccer on the global stage. Pelé's achievements made Brazil a respected and feared opponent in international soccer, a status it still holds proudly today!

Beyond the soccer field, Pelé became a symbol of Brazilian culture. His charm and humbleness made him a beloved figure worldwide. Wherever he went, he proudly shared Brazilian culture and soccer, bringing people together through the universal language of soccer. Pelé's influence went far beyond the pitch. He was invited to meet world leaders, appeared on TV, and even had songs written about him. He used his fame to promote not just soccer but also positive values like sportsmanship, dedication, and perseverance. Pelé's impact was so profound that he became a symbol of hope and pride for Brazil, a country that had faced its fair share of challenges. Through his actions and words, Pelé showed the world the beauty of Brazilian culture and the spirit of its people.

MONEY TROUBLES

Pelé's story isn't just about dazzling dribbles and spectacular goals; it's also about fighting money problems, even after he started his pro career. You might think that all his money worries disappeared once he signed his first contract. But that wasn't true. Despite his rising fame, Pelé and his family still faced money worries. The early days of his career were marked by smaller paychecks, and the wealth that soccer promised was slow to arrive. It's like getting your first job and realizing that your paycheck doesn't stretch as far as you'd hoped. Pelé had to be smart about his money, ensuring his family's basic needs were met first.

As Pelé's career continued, he began to think beyond just playing soccer. He realized that he needed to secure his family's future. Instead of spending all his money, Pelé wisely put his money towards businesses and real estate. He bought houses and started small businesses, understanding that these investments would grow over time. Think of it like planting a garden. You sow the seeds, water them, and patiently wait for them to bloom. Pelé's investments were his seeds, and over time, they provided him with a steady income, ensuring he would have money long after his playing days were over.

But Pelé's investments weren't just about himself. He also wanted to give back to his family and community. He supported his parents and siblings with his money, ensuring they had comfortable lives. Beyond his family, Pelé was deeply committed to helping his community. He funded local sports programs, allowing young kids to play soccer and dream big, just like he once did. Picture a local soccer field filled with kids running around, laughing, and honing their skills, all because Pelé believed in giving back. His generosity had a ripple effect, inspiring others to invest in their communities and support the next generation of soccer stars.

Pelé didn't stop providing financial support; he also became a strong leader for smart money choices among athletes. He often spoke about the importance of understanding finances, making wise investments, and planning for the future. For many young athletes, the sudden amount of money can be overwhelming, and without proper guidance, it can quickly disappear. Pelé used his platform to educate fellow athletes, encouraging them to think long-term and make smart financial decisions.

Pelé's advocacy for financial literacy was a mission to guide and inspire others. His efforts paved the way for many athletes to take control of their finances, ensuring they could lead comfortable lives and continue contributing to their communities long after their playing days were over. Pelé's role as a financial mentor added another dimension to his legacy, demonstrating that true success is not just about on-field achievements but also about managing and sharing resources off the field.

LEGACY

Besides being a soccer superstar, Pelé was committed to charity, giving back and blessing others. He worked tirelessly with organizations like UNICEF, using his fame to support various social causes. Picture Pelé, not just as a soccer star but as someone who genuinely cared about making the world a better place. He focused on children's education and health, traveling to different countries to raise awareness and support. He did more than give his money; he actively helped out and visited projects to help others. His involvement showed that he understood the power of his position and wanted to use it for good. Pelé's efforts in charity inspired many to follow his example, proving that even a soccer star could make a significant impact off the field.

Pelé's legacy is a powerful source of inspiration for young athletes and individuals, teaching them to overcome their own challenges. His life is a guide on how to achieve dreams despite facing tough obstacles. Schools and soccer academies often use his story to teach lessons like hard work, dedication, and strength. Every time a young player steps onto the field, they carry a bit of Pelé's spirit with them, reminding them that no matter what obstacles they face, they can always find a way to succeed if they believe in themselves.

In wrapping up this chapter, it's clear that Pelé's impact goes far beyond the soccer field. His role as an ambassador, his charities, his status as a cultural icon, and his inspiring ability make his legacy truly remarkable. Pelé showed the world that soccer is more than just a game; it's a way to connect, inspire, and create positive change. His story is one of resilience, generosity, and hope, setting the stage for the next chapter, where we'll explore the incredible journey of Cristiano Ronaldo, another soccer legend who has inspired millions with his talent and determination.

Neymar

CHAPTER FOUR
NEYMAR: EMBRACING INDIVIDUALITY AND SELF-EXPRESSION

"I always try to be myself. I never try to be someone else."

NEYMAR

Picture this: a small town in Brazil with narrow, winding streets filled with the sounds of laughter and the rhythmic thud of a soccer ball being kicked around. It's hot, the sun is blazing, and kids are running barefoot on the dusty roads, dreaming of becoming the next big soccer star. Among them is a young boy named Neymar da Silva Santos Júnior, or simply Neymar. From the moment he could walk, Neymar had a soccer ball at his feet. His story is all about passion, family support, and a unique style that would one day make him one of the most recognizable soccer players in the world.

Neymar was born in Mogi das Cruzes, a town in São Paulo, Brazil. Soccer wasn't just a game for Neymar; it was a way of life. From the age of four, he was already showing signs of his incredible talent. He would play soccer with his friends in the streets and on makeshift fields, using anything they could find as goalposts.

Imagine being a little kid and having this unstoppable drive to play soccer every single day. That was Neymar. He would spend hours practicing his dribbling, shooting, and tricks, often losing track of time because he was so immersed in the game. His love for soccer was evident to everyone around him, and it was clear that this kid was something special.

Neymar's family played a huge role in nurturing his talent. His father, Neymar Santos Sr., was a former soccer player himself and understood the importance of supporting his son's dreams. He would often take Neymar to local matches and training sessions, offering guidance and encouragement. Neymar's mother, Nadine, was equally supportive, always making sure her son had everything he needed to pursue his passion. The family didn't have a lot of money, but what they lacked in finances, they made up for with love and support. They believed in Neymar's potential and were willing to make sacrifices to help him succeed. It's like having your own personal cheerleading squad, always there to lift you up and push you forward.

As Neymar grew older, he began to develop a unique playing style that set him apart from other kids. He wasn't just playing soccer; he was creating art on the field. His dribbling was mesmerizing, his footwork was dazzling, and his creativity knew no bounds. Neymar had a flair for the dramatic, often pulling off tricks and moves that left spectators in awe. He would practice endlessly, perfecting his skills and experimenting with new techniques. It wasn't just about scoring goals for Neymar; it was about expressing himself through the game. His style was flashy, bold, and unapologetically unique. Imagine watching a magician perform tricks with a soccer ball— that was what it felt like to watch Neymar play.

Locally, Neymar's talent did not go unnoticed. By the time he was just six years old, he was already turning heads in his community. Local clubs and coaches saw his potential and were eager to have him join their teams. Neymar started playing for Portuguesa Santista, a local youth team, where he quickly became the star player. His performances on the field were nothing short of spectacular, and people began to take notice. Coaches marveled at his skill, and fans came to watch him play, even at such a young age. Neymar's name started spreading, and he became somewhat of a local celebrity. His talent was undeniable, and everyone who saw him play knew that he was destined for greatness.

Reflect on your own passions. What activities make you lose track of time because you love them so much? Think about how you can develop your own unique style in whatever you do, just like Neymar did with soccer. Grab a journal and write down your thoughts. What makes you unique? How can you express yourself through your favorite activities?

Neymar's early life is a testament to the power of passion, family support, and individuality. From playing in the streets of Mogi das Cruzes to dazzling local clubs with his skills, Neymar's journey began with a love for the game and the unwavering support of his family. His unique style and incredible talent set him apart, earning him recognition and admiration from an early age. Neymar's story is a reminder that with passion, support, and a bit of creativity, you can achieve amazing things. So, next time you're out playing soccer or pursuing your own dreams, remember Neymar's journey and let it inspire you to embrace your individuality and express yourself in everything you do.

RISING TO FAME

Neymar's professional debut with Santos FC was like fireworks on New Year's Eve. He was only 17, but he played with the spirit of a seasoned pro. His first match was a peek into the future, showing what was to come. Neymar dazzled the crowd with his speed, footwork, and creativity on the ball. He wasn't just playing; he was putting on a show. He kept getting better with every game, scoring goals that left everyone shocked. Santos FC quickly realized they had a gem on their hands. Neymar's success at Santos set the stage for his future career, making him one of the most talked-about young players in Brazil.

It was a whole new ball game when Neymar moved to Europe to play for FC Barcelona. Imagine moving to a new country where you barely speak the language, all while the entire world is watching. That's the kind of pressure Neymar faced. But instead of crumbling, he succeeded. The excitement of joining one of the biggest clubs in the world was mixed with challenges. He had to adapt to a new style of play, different weather, and a new culture. But Neymar took it all in stride. He formed a powerful trio with Lionel Messi and Luis Suárez, creating one of soccer's most lethal attacking lines. Every match was like a class in soccer mastery. Neymar's performances in Europe elevated his game to new heights.

Worldwide fame came knocking on Neymar's door when he started making waves in Europe. His incredible performances for both Santos FC and FC Barcelona caught the attention of soccer fans worldwide. Suddenly, Neymar was more than just a Brazilian star; he was a global icon. His skill set, flair, and charisma made him a fan favorite. People from all parts of the world tuned in to watch him play. Neymar was everywhere—on TV, in magazines, and on social media. His fame wasn't just about his talent; it was about his ability to charm and connect with fans across the world.

Balancing the expectations and pressures of being a young star was hard for Neymar. Imagine having millions of people expect you to be perfect every time you step onto the field. The weight of those expectations can be scary. But Neymar managed it with grace and belief. He understood that he couldn't please everyone and that mistakes were part of the game. He focused on what he could control—his performance, his training, and his mindset. Whenever the pressure mounted, he turned to his family and close friends for support. They kept him content, reminding him of where he came from and why he started playing soccer in the first place. This balance allowed Neymar to stay true to himself and continue to perform at the highest level.

Neymar's rise to fame is a story of talent, hard work, and resilience. From his debut with Santos FC to his move to Europe and international recognition, every step showed his dedication and love for the game. Balancing the pressures of fame with his passion for soccer, Neymar showed the world that staying true to yourself is possible while reaching for the stars.

CELEBRATING INDIVIDUALITY

Neymar isn't like most soccer players. When he's on the field, it's almost like watching an artist at work. His clever dribbling skills are something special. Picture him threading through defenders as if they're mere cones. His feet move so quickly that it's like the ball is glued to his shoes. Neymar has an incredible skill to change direction in a split second, leaving his opponents baffled and the crowd roaring in excitement. His signature dribbling isn't just about getting past players; it's about doing it with style and flair.

He brings a unique blend of speed, control, and creativity, making every game he plays a must-watch event.

But Neymar doesn't stop at dribbling. He's known for his showmanship, pulling off tricks and flicks that most players wouldn't even dare to try. Imagine performing a rainbow flick in the middle of a high-stakes match—flipping the ball over your head and your opponent's head in one smooth motion. That's the kind of fearless skill Neymar brings to the table. His tricks aren't just for show; they're helpful and often lead to scoring chances. Fans love him for this. Every time he steps onto the field, you can sense the excitement. Will he pull off a new trick? Will he do something we've never seen before? His showmanship delights audiences worldwide, making him a favorite among soccer fans and casual viewers.

Of course, not everyone loves Neymar's flashy style. Critics often argue his tricks and flair are excessive or disrespectful to the game. But Neymar handles this criticism with a calm, collected demeanor. Instead of letting the negative comments get to him, he uses them as motivation to keep improving and pushing the limits of what's possible on the field. He understands that not everyone will appreciate his style, but he remains true to himself. He knows that staying true to his style and personality sets him apart, and he doesn't let anyone take that away.

Neymar's individuality doesn't just shine on the field; it inspires young players to embrace their uniqueness as well. Imagine being a kid, watching Neymar play, and thinking, "I want to be like him." His creativity and flair encourage young athletes to develop their own style and not be afraid to stand out. Neymar shows that soccer isn't just about following the rules; it's about expressing yourself and having fun. His influence reaches far beyond the pro leagues, touching the lives of countless young players who see him as a role model. Neymar's story teaches them that it's okay to be different, to take risks, and to play the game their way. His impact is a powerful motivator, inspiring young athletes to be their best version.

Just like Neymar, you have the power to captivate and inspire others by being yourself. Neymar's signature dribbling, showmanship, and ability to handle criticism all point to one thing: his commitment to individuality. He's not just playing soccer; he's making a statement. His unique style not only defines his career but also serves as a beacon of inspiration for young athletes everywhere. Neymar shows us that being true to yourself is the key to unlocking your full potential, both on and off the field.

INFLUENCE BEYOND SOCCER

Neymar isn't just a star on the soccer field; he's also a trendsetter in the fashion world. You would easily catch him walking down the runway of a high-end fashion show. Neymar's sense of style is bold and undeniably cool. He's often seen wearing the latest clothes and designer suits and even experimenting with different hairstyles. His influence in fashion goes beyond just wearing clothes; it's about expressing himself and pushing the boundaries of what's considered stylish. Neymar's fashion choices are as daring as his dribbles, and they resonate with fans who love to see what he'll wear next. He's worked with major brands like Nike and Puma, launching his own clothing lines that reflect his unique style. For many young fans, Neymar is a fashion icon, showing them that taking risks and being confident in their skin is okay.

In addition to his fashion, Neymar's heart is as big as his talent, and he uses his platform to give back through various generous efforts. He established the Neymar Jr. Institute, a non-profit organization that provides academic options and sports programs for poorer children in Brazil. The institute aims to create a positive impact on the lives of these kids, giving them hope and chances they might not have had otherwise. His generosity and commitment to helping others show that being a true star means using your influence to make the world a better place.

Neymar's cultural impact is immense, surpassing the world of sports and reaching into popular culture. Think about it: he's not just known for his soccer skills; he's a household name recognized by people who might not even watch soccer. Neymar has appeared in music videos and movies and has even been a character in video games. His charm makes him a natural fit for entertainment. He's collaborated with artists, starred in commercials, and even hosted his own reality show. Neymar's presence in popular culture helps bridge the gap between sports and entertainment, making him a versatile and influential figure. His ability to connect with diverse audiences and his impact on different aspects of culture highlight his status as a global icon.

INSPIRATIONAL FIGURE

Neymar's story is a powerful message of self-belief. Imagine being constantly told that you're too flashy or different or that your style won't work. For Neymar, those criticisms were like fuel. He believed in his unique way of playing and stuck with it, no matter what others said. This determined self-confidence is what sets him apart and makes him a role model for so many. His story tells kids everywhere that it's okay to be different. In fact, it's those differences that can make you special. When Neymar steps onto the field, he's not just playing soccer; he's expressing who he is. Neymar's belief in himself shows that being true to who you are can lead to greatness.

Neymar's influence extends far beyond Brazil. His impact on soccer fans and aspiring athletes around the world is massive. He's inspired millions to pick up a soccer ball and give it their all. Young athletes look up to him, not just for his talent but for his dedication and flair. They see him as proof that hard work and individuality can lead to global success. Neymar's global reach makes him a symbol of hope for many who aspire to make their mark in the world.

Through public appearances and media, Neymar's influence only grows stronger. He's not just a face on a soccer field; he's a voice that people listen to. Whether through interviews, commercials, or public speaking events, Neymar uses his platform to inspire and motivate. He talks about the importance of staying true to oneself, working hard, and never giving up. His words resonate with people of all ages, encouraging them to chase their dreams with the same passion he has. Neymar's public presence isn't just about advertising brands; it's about sharing a message of resilience and self-expression. He reaches out to fans, making them feel valued and appreciated. This connection makes his influence even more profound, as people see him as someone who genuinely cares about making a difference.

Neymar's story of self-belief, global influence, public speaking, and lasting legacy makes him an inspirational figure for young athletes and fans everywhere. His message is clear: be yourself, work hard, and never let anyone dull your shine. Neymar's impact is felt far and wide, making him a beacon of hope and inspiration for all who dare to dream. As we move forward, we'll explore the journey of another soccer legend who has used his platform to unite a nation and inspire millions: Didier Drogba.

Activity: Embracing Your Inner Neymar

Neymar's story is all about individuality—expressing yourself boldly, both on and off the field. Think about a time when you let your true self shine, even if it made you stand out from the crowd. Maybe it was through your style, a talent you shared, or an idea you had. How did it feel to embrace your uniqueness? Did others respond positively, or was it challenging to stay confident?

Write about this moment in your journal. Reflect on how you can continue to celebrate what makes you, you. How can you balance being true to yourself while also working with others as a team? What does individuality mean to you, and how can it inspire you to achieve your goals?

Neymar's journey reminds us that being unique is a strength, not a weakness. Neymar shows us that individuality can inspire others, whether it's his creative moves on the field or his bold personality. As you think about your own life, consider how you can use your talents and authenticity to leave your mark, while staying connected to the people and teams around you.

LET'S MOTIVATE KIDS EVERYWHERE!

Hey there, young soccer stars!

You know that awesome feeling when you make a perfect pass, setting up your teammate to score the winning goal? That's what I'm asking you to do right now—but off the field! You might not get the goal for yourself, but you can help someone else find this book and be inspired by these incredible soccer stories.

Our goal is to motivate kids everywhere with stories of challenges, victories, and lessons learned on the pitch. Every goal, every match, and every season teaches something valuable, and we want to share these lessons with as many young players as possible.

Here's where you come in. A lot of people decide what books to read based on reviews. By asking your parents, teacher, or coach to leave a review for this book, you'll be making the perfect assist.

Think of it this way: your review could help...

- Another young player learn how to bounce back from a tough loss.
- A friend find the courage to try out for their school soccer team.
- Someone your age feel inspired to chase their dreams, just like their favorite soccer star.

And the best part? It doesn't cost anything and takes less than a minute! Just scan the QR code below or use the link to leave your review:

QR code / Review Link:

If you love being a team player, this is your chance to shine. Welcome to the squad! I can't wait to share more cool soccer stories, skills, and life lessons in the next chapters.

Thanks a million for your help. You're not just a reader; you're a playmaker.

Chris Villanueva

P.S. – Remember, sharing something valuable makes you a star in someone else's eyes. If you think this book can inspire another kid, why not pass it along? Just like a great assist, it could lead to an unforgettable goal. 📱⚽

Rapinoe

CHAPTER FIVE
MEGAN RAPINOE: VOICE FOR EQUALITY AND CAPTAIN AMERICA

"I was made exactly the way I was meant to be made in who I am and my personality and the way I was born."

MEGAN RAPINOE

On the biggest stage in the world, under the bright lights, millions of eyes watch your every move. Your heart is pounding, your teammates are counting on you, and the weight of expectations is heavy on your shoulders. This was Megan Rapinoe during the 2019 Women's World Cup. From the moment the tournament started, Megan was not just a player; she was a leader, a symbol of resilience and spirit for her team and fans around the globe.

The 2019 World Cup in France was an epic wonder, and Megan Rapinoe stood at its center. Picture the roar of the crowd, the sea of flags waving in the stands, and the intense focus of players ready to give their all. Megan led the US Women's National Team with an amazing blend of skill, confidence, and charisma. Her role wasn't just about playing well; it was about inspiring her teammates to play their best. Every time she took the field, she brought an energy that spread around, lifting the spirits of everyone around her.

Throughout the tournament, Megan's performance was nothing short of spectacular. She scored six goals, including some of the most critical ones that propelled the team to victory. One of the most memorable moments was her penalty kick against Spain in the Round of 16. Imagine the pressure: a knockout game, a tied score, and it all comes down to Megan. She steps up, calm and focused, and delivers a powerful shot that hits the back of the net, securing the win for America. This goal wasn't just a point on the scoreboard; it was a statement of her poise under pressure.

As the tournament went on, Megan continued to shine. In the quarterfinals against France, she scored both goals in a 2-1 victory, showcasing her knack for rising to the occasion when it mattered most. Her first goal came from a free kick that sliced through the defense like a hot knife through butter. The second was a brilliant finish following a fast-paced counterattack. These moments weren't just about the goals themselves; they were about the leadership and confidence she exuded, inspiring her teammates to follow her and believe in themselves.

By the end of the tournament, Megan was rewarded with the Golden Boot, awarded to the top scorer, and the Golden Ball, given to the best player of the tournament. Winning the Golden Boot was a testament to her incredible ability to find the back of the net. The Golden Ball recognized her as the best player overall, highlighting her leadership, skill, and impact throughout the tournament.

Megan's leadership on the field was obvious in how she interacted with her teammates. She was always there with kind words, a pat on the back, or a rallying cry to keep spirits high. She knew the importance of unity and teamwork, often taking the time to uplift and support her fellow players. Another memorable moment was during the semifinal against England. With the game tied and tensions high, Megan was seen motivating her teammates, reminding them of their strength and ability. They listened to her well, and the team won 2-1, securing their place in the final.

Her leadership extended beyond words; it was also about setting an example through her actions. Megan's work ethic, determination, and passion were visible every time she stepped onto the pitch. She played every game with the same intensity and commitment, never letting up for a moment. This kind of leadership inspired her teammates to give their best, knowing that their captain was doing the same. In the final against the Netherlands, Megan opened the scoring with a clinical penalty, setting the tone for a 2-0 victory and securing the World Cup title for the US.

Megan Rapinoe's journey through the 2019 World Cup is a masterclass in leadership, skill, and resilience. Her ability to inspire and uplift her teammates, along with her remarkable skills, made her an unforgettable figure in the tournament.

VOICE FOR FAIRNESS AND EQUALITY

Megan Rapinoe isn't just a legend on the soccer field; she's also a fierce supporter of fairness and equality. She dares to stand up for what she believes in, even when it's not the easiest path. She's used her popularity to speak out on issues that matter, ensuring that everyone, regardless of gender, race, or background, is treated fairly. One of her most significant efforts has been fighting for equal pay in women's sports. Megan has been vocal about the unfair pay between male and female athletes, especially in soccer. She's clear that women deserve the same respect, opportunities, and money as their male counterparts.

The equal pay movement in women's sports has gained much traction, largely thanks to Megan's actions. Imagine being part of a team that has won multiple World Cups and Olympic medals, yet you are being paid less than your teammates because of their gender or race. That's the reality Megan and her teammates faced. But instead of just accepting it, they decided to fight back. Megan and her US Women's National Team teammates chose to complain directly to the Soccer Federation. This bold move showed this issue to the world, sparking conversations and support around the world. Megan's role in this fight has been crucial. She's not just advocating for herself or her team; she's standing up for all female athletes who deserve to be treated fairly for their hard work.

Megan's public statements have had a massive impact on the movement for fairness. She says that the fight for equal pay isn't just about money; it's about respect and honor. One of her most powerful statements came during the 2019 World Cup when she said, "We have to be better. We have to love more and hate less. We got to listen more and talk less. We got to know that this is everybody's responsibility." These words echoed with people from all over the world, showing that the fight for fairness goes beyond sports. Megan's ability to speak her thoughts and stand firm in her beliefs has inspired many to join the cause and demand change.

Megan's involvement with various organizations and movements further highlights her commitment to making a difference. Imagine being part of a team fighting for justice and equality, knowing that someone like Megan is in your corner, using her voice and platform to bring attention to your cause.

Megan's voice for fairness and equality has made her a beacon of hope and inspiration for many. Her influence goes beyond just words; they're about taking action and making a real difference. Through her fight for equal pay, her powerful public statements, and her involvement with various organizations, Megan has shown that one person can spark a movement and inspire others to join the fight for a fairer and better world.

BEING A TEAM LEADER

Megan Rapinoe's leadership style is all about creating a strong, supportive, and resilient team. Picture being part of a team where everyone has each other's back, no matter what. That's the kind of aura Megan creates. She understands that soccer isn't just about individual talent; it's about how well the team works together. Her leadership is marked by her ability to become friends with each player, making everyone feel valued and important. Whether it's a word of encouragement during practice or a pep talk before a big game, Megan knows how to lift her teammates' spirits and keep them motivated. She's like the glue that holds the team together, making sure that everyone is on the same page and working towards a common goal.

Creating unity within a team can be hard, but Megan has a gift for it. One of her techniques is leading by example. She always gives her best, whether it's during practice sessions or in actual games. Her hard work inspires her teammates to do the same. Megan also knows the importance of open communication. She encourages her teammates to speak up, share their thoughts, and express their concerns. This open discussion helps to build trust and understanding within the team. Megan also organizes team bonding activities, like dinners or outings, where players can relax and get to know each other outside of soccer. These help to strengthen the bonds between teammates, creating a positive team culture.

Handling pressure is something Megan excels very well at. Let's say she has a crucial match with the score tied and only a few minutes left on the clock. The pressure is immense. But Megan remains calm and composed. She knows that losing her cool won't help. Instead, she focuses on what she can control—her mindset. Megan uses techniques to stay focused, picturing herself making successful plays before they happen. She shares this approach with her teammates, helping them stay calm and focused under pressure. Megan's ability to handle high-pressure situations with grace and confidence is proof of her mental strength and resilience.

Megan's role as a mentor to younger players is a big aspect of her leadership. She understands that the future of the team depends on the younger members. Megan takes the time to mentor and guide them, sharing her experiences and offering advice. She's always there to listen, provide feedback, and cheer them on. It's incredibly motivating and helps to build confidence. Megan's mentorship fosters a sense of belonging and encourages younger players to strive for greatness. She's not just a leader on the field; she's a mentor who genuinely cares about the growth and development of her teammates.

Megan's impact on team dynamics goes beyond just her actions; it's also about the positive energy she brings to the team. Her enthusiasm and passion for the game are contagious. She knows how to keep the mood light and fun, even during intense training sessions or high-pressure matches. Her sense of humor and playful nature help to create a relaxed and enjoyable atmosphere, allowing her teammates to perform at their best. Megan's ability to balance seriousness with fun is one of the reasons why she's such an effective leader. She knows when to push hard and when to let loose, creating a balanced and harmonious team environment.

Megan Rapinoe's leadership qualities are shown in her supportive and inclusive approach, which fosters a strong and resilient team environment where every player feels valued and motivated. Megan's ability to inspire and uplift her teammates is a testament to her incredible leadership skills, making her an invaluable asset to the US Women's National Team.

PERSONAL JOURNEY AND CHALLENGES

Megan Rapinoe's story isn't just about her wins on the soccer field; it's also about the obstacles she's faced and overcome, both personally and professionally. Imagine being at the peak of your career and then suddenly sidelined by a devastating knee injury. That happened to Megan in 2015 when she hurt her knee badly during a training session. This injury could have ended her career. But instead of letting it break her spirit, Megan faced the long, tough healing process with determination. She worked hard, not just to get back to where she was but to come back even stronger. Her strength in the face of such a setback is proof of her powerful spirit. In addition to the physical side of her recovery, she knew staying positive was the key to it all.

We just talked about how Megan would speak out and fight for fairness outside of sports, making her a target for critics. Some disagree with her views or think she should "just stick to sports." But Megan doesn't let the negativity get to her. She understands that standing up for what you believe in will always attract criticism. Instead of shying away, she uses it as motivation to keep pushing forward. Her ability to stay focused and maintain her integrity, even when under intense scrutiny, is remarkable. She has developed a thick skin and a sharp sense of self, knowing that her voice is powerful and necessary.

Megan's resilience and determination are key factors in her success. She's faced numerous obstacles, from injuries to public backlash, and has always come out stronger on the other side. Think about when things haven't gone your way and you've felt like giving up. Megan has been there, too. But she's shown that endurance pays off. She approaches every challenge with the mindset that it's an opportunity to grow and learn. Whether it's recovering from an injury, dealing with criticism, or fighting for equality, Megan tackles each hurdle head-on. This determination has not only made her a better player but also a stronger person. Her mantra could be, "Fall seven times, stand up eight."

These experiences have contributed to Megan's personal growth and leadership. Every challenge she's faced has taught her valuable lessons about resilience, empathy, and the importance of staying true to oneself. These experiences have made her a more compassionate leader, someone who understands the importance of supporting and uplifting others. She's learned that true leadership isn't just about being the best player on the field; it's about being there for your teammates and helping them through their own challenges.

Megan's personal growth is evident in how she leads both on and off the field. Her title of captain is more than just a title; she embodies the role through her actions and attitude. Her challenges have made her more understanding and patient, qualities that are essential for effective leadership. She knows what it's like to struggle, to face seemingly insurmountable odds, and to come out stronger. This perspective allows her to connect with her teammates on a deeper level, offering support and guidance when they need it most. Megan's journey is a powerful example of how facing and overcoming challenges can lead to profound personal growth and make you a more effective and inspiring leader.

Through all these experiences, Megan Rapinoe has shown that challenges are not roadblocks but growth opportunities. Her resilience, determination, and ability to handle public scrutiny have defined her career and made her a role model for many.

INSPIRATIONAL FIGURE WORLDWIDE

Megan Rapinoe stands tall as a global role model, not just for her soccer skills but for her fearless approach to addressing social issues. Imagine being an athlete and having the courage to speak out about things that matter, even when it's risky. That's Megan. She's the kind of person who doesn't just kick a ball; she kicks down barriers. She leads by example. She shows that being a great athlete is more than just talent; it's also about having the guts to stand up for what's right.

Throughout her career, Megan has received numerous awards and recognitions highlighting her impact on and off the field. She was named the Best FIFA Women's Player in 2019, a famous award that recognizes her outstanding contributions to soccer.

Megan's influence extends beyond the soccer field, especially through her public speaking and media presence. Picture her standing on stage, confident and articulate, sharing her experiences and insights with audiences around the world. She's been a speaker at major events, including the Women's March and the Forbes Women's Summit. Her speeches are always impactful and filled with passion and authenticity. She doesn't just talk about her success; she talks about her struggles, beliefs, and vision for a better world. Her words relate to people from all walks of life, inspiring them to take action and make a difference. Megan's ability to connect with audiences through her public speaking is a testament to her influence and commitment to driving positive change.

Megan's ongoing legacy is something that will continue to inspire future generations. Imagine young girls and boys growing up, looking up to Megan not just as a soccer star but as a symbol of strength and advocacy. Her efforts have paved the way for more inclusive and equitable sports environments, and her influence will be felt for years to come. Her story is a powerful reminder that true greatness comes from using your platform to uplift and empower others.

Megan Rapinoe's role as a global figure, her numerous awards, her impactful public speaking, and her lasting legacy all highlight her extraordinary influence. She's not just a soccer player; she's a symbol of hope and a force for change. As we move forward, we'll explore the journey of another soccer legend who has used his platform to unite a nation and inspire millions: Didier Drogba.

Drogba

CHAPTER SIX
DIDIER DROGBA: UNITING A TORN COUNTRY

"I have won many trophies in my time, but nothing will ever top helping win the battle for peace in my country."

DIDIER DROGBA

Let's now discuss the story of a young boy in the Ivory Coast, Africa. His story is one of resilience, determination, and the incredible power of sport to bring people together. This boy who would become a soccer hero is named Didier Drogba.

Drogba was born in Abidjan, the largest city in Ivory Coast, where life was anything but easy. His family didn't have much, but they shared a love for soccer. Drogba's father, Albert, and mother, Clotilde, believed in their son's talent. They knew that soccer could be his ticket to a better life, but they also knew that staying in Ivory Coast wasn't going to give him the opportunities he needed. So, at the young age of five, Didier was sent to live with his uncle Michel in France, a country known for its strong soccer clubs and training facilities. Imagine the sacrifice of a family, sending their young son to a foreign land, all in the hope of chasing a dream.

Adjusting to life in France was hard for young Didier. He missed his family terribly and struggled with the cultural differences. The weather was colder, the language was different, and the food wasn't anything like the spicy dishes he loved back home. School was tough, too, and sometimes he felt like he didn't belong. But his love for soccer was stubborn. On the field, he felt at home. He could let his feet do the talking, and his talent quickly caught the attention of local coaches. Despite the homesickness and the challenges of adapting to a new culture, Drogba's love for soccer was his constant source of comfort and motivation.

As Drogba grew older, his skills on the field continued to improve. His breakthrough came when he joined Levallois SC, a club in the suburbs of Paris. Here, his talent shone brightly, and it wasn't long before scouts from bigger clubs started to take notice. This was a turning point in Drogba's life. He moved on to play for Le Mans, a professional club in France's second division. His performances were impressive, and he quickly became one of the team's standout players. But even as his career began to take off, Drogba never forgot his family's sacrifices. Every goal he scored was a step closer to repaying their faith in him.

Then came the big move that would change everything. In 2004, Didier Drogba was signed by Chelsea FC, one of the top clubs in the English Premier League. This transfer marked the beginning of his rise to soccer superstar. Picture the excitement and pressure of moving to one of the biggest soccer leagues in the world. Drogba was ready. He embraced the challenge straight on. At Chelsea, he quickly became a fan favorite, known for his powerful shots, incredible headers, and relentless determination. On the field, he was electrifying, and his ability to score crucial goals in important matches earned him a reputation as one of the best strikers in the world.

Joining Chelsea allowed Drgoba to proudly represent his home country on a world stage. Every time he scored a goal or lifted a trophy, it wasn't just a victory for him; it was a victory for Ivory Coast. Drogba's success made his country proud and inspired countless young kids back home to dream big. His journey from the dusty streets of Abidjan to the grand stadiums of Europe was a beacon of hope, showing that with hard work, dedication, and a bit of support, anything is possible.

DIDIER'S CEASEFIRE PLEA

Didier Drogba is more than a soccer player, and he proved that when he did something that brought peace to a country and stopped a war. It was 2005, and Ivory Coast was torn apart by a brutal civil war, which meant two sides of the same country were fighting each other. The country needed more than just a hero on the soccer field; it needed a voice to bring everyone together. Drogba knew how much people listened to him through cameras, so he took a deep breath and spoke directly, pleading for a ceasefire. His words were powerful, heartfelt, and honest. "Ivorians, we beg you, on our knees, to put down your weapons and hold elections," he said. Imagine seeing your favorite soccer star not scoring a goal but kneeling and asking for peace. It was a moment that transcended sports and touched the hearts of millions.

The impact of Drogba's plea was quick and powerful, providing a sense of unity that everyone had been waiting for. His words were heard from people across the nation, from everyday citizens to the fighting soldiers. Soldiers who had been fighting each other suddenly saw a new path forward. They heard Drogba's call for peace and were moved by his words. His plea was broadcast on national television, reaching homes and hearts all over Ivory Coast. The response was overwhelming. People took to the streets not to protest but to celebrate the possibility of peace. It was as if a heavy cloud had been lifted, and a new sense of hope lived. Even the soldiers, who had been locked in a bitter struggle, began to see their need for peace.

Soccer played a huge role in uniting people together during this time of conflict. The national team, known as the Elephants, was a symbol of pride for all Ivorians, regardless of their political or ethnic background. When the Elephants played, the nation paused its conflicts, if only for 90 minutes, to cheer for their team. Drogba, as the captain and star player, embodied this unity. He wasn't just a player; he was a symbol of what Ivory Coast could be —a nation united by a shared passion. The power of soccer to bridge divides and bring people together was never more clear than during this period. It showed that a shared love for the game could foster hope and unity even in the darkest times.

Following Drogba's emotional plea, the warring soldiers agreed to a temporary ceasefire. It was a significant, albeit fragile, step towards peace. The end of the fighting allowed aid to reach affected areas. It opened the door for dialogue between the fighting parties. For the first time in years, there was hope that peace could be achieved. Drogba's influence went beyond just stopping the fighting; it paved the way for peace talks and a more stable future. The temporary peace was a testament to the power of one individual's voice to effect change. It showed that hope and unity could prevail even in the face of seemingly impossible challenges.

INFLUENCE THROUGH SUCCESS

Didier Drogba's global success was like a megaphone for the issues facing Ivory Coast. As he scored goals and won matches, he wasn't just making headlines in sports sections; he was drawing global attention to his home country. Drogba knew that because he played in front of millions of fans, he had the power to shine a spotlight on important topics going on in the world. Drogba used his platform to raise awareness about the civil war and the need for peace and unity. His success on the field gave him a voice that resonated far beyond the stadiums. People around the world started to take notice of the Ivory Coast, not just as a country in turmoil but as a nation with potential and hope.

Playing for Chelsea in the Premier League, Drogba achieved feats that only a few could dream of. He became known for his clutch performances, especially in big games, where he would perform very well in the final minutes of a game. Picture this: it's the final of the UEFA Champions League in 2012, and the match is tied. Drogba steps up and scores a decisive penalty, leading Chelsea to their first-ever Champions League title. This was both a victory for the club and a personal triumph that rose him into global stardom. During his time at Chelsea, Drogba won multiple Premier League titles, FA Cups, and League Cups. His ability to rise to the occasion when it mattered most made him a legend. Each trophy he lifted boosted his status and brought more attention to the causes he cared about.

Advocacy for peace became a cornerstone of Drogba's life, both on and off the field. He realized that his soccer success gave him a unique platform to promote peace and unity. Drogba didn't just play for the love of the game; he played to unite his country. After his plea for a ceasefire, he continued to advocate for peace through various initiatives. He met with political leaders, participated in peace talks, and supported efforts to rebuild war-torn communities. Even though he was just considered a soccer player, that did not stop him from speaking to whoever he could to make a positive change. His advocacy efforts extended beyond speeches and meetings. He invested in projects to heal the nation and foster long-term stability. Drogba's commitment to peace showed that soccer could be more than just a sport; it could be a force for good.

Drogba's influence through his international success, Premier League achievements, global recognition, and advocacy for peace paints a picture of a man who used his talents not just for personal gain but for the betterment of his country. His story is a powerful reminder that success comes with responsibility and that even the brightest stars can shine a light on the darkest corners.

NATIONAL PEACE

Didier Drogba's actions in peace-building didn't stop after he made his famous call for peace on television. He took his commitment to peace a step further by organizing the national team's "peace tour." They were a group of gifted soccer players that traveled across the country, not just to play matches but to spread a message of unity and hope. They visited various parts of the Ivory Coast, playing friendly matches and spending time with local communities. These tours used the power of soccer to bring people together, showing that despite their differences, they could all come together to build peace. The national team's presence in these regions was a powerful symbol of unity, demonstrating that if they could come together for the love of the game, so could the nation.

This was a great example of Drogba's influence and how it extended beyond the soccer field. He even actively spoke with government leaders to promote peace. Picture Drogba, not in his soccer kit, but in a suit, sitting across from politicians and military leaders, discussing ways to bring peace to his country. His meetings weren't just for show; they were heartfelt conversations where he used his influence and respect to bridge gaps and foster understanding. Drogba's ability to connect with people from all walks of life made him a unique person who could fix disagreements between others. His efforts in these meetings played a big role in promoting conversation and understanding, making the way for lasting peace.

Working in the community was another cornerstone of Drogba's peace-building efforts. He understood that real change starts at the grassroots level. So, he made it a point to engage with local communities, organizing events that fostered unity and cooperation. Imagine Drogba visiting a small village, playing soccer with the kids, and talking to the elders about the importance of peace. His presence in these communities was inspiring. He wasn't just a distant celebrity; he was someone who cared deeply about their well-being. He listened to their stories, understood their struggles, and encouraged them to work together for a better future. Drogba's community outreach efforts showed that peace isn't just about stopping the fighting; it's about building relationships and fostering a sense of belonging and unity.

Drogba's commitment to peace continued for a long time. He was involved in long-term projects and ambitions to maintain peace and stability in Ivory Coast. One of his significant contributions was the establishment of the Didier Drogba Foundation, which focuses on health, education, and social development. Through his foundation, Drogba funded the construction of hospitals, schools, and community centers, providing essential services and opportunities to those in need. You would see a new hospital being built in a remote area, helping those who were sick in places where people previously had no medical help. That's the kind of impact Drogba's foundation had. These long-term initiatives were crucial in addressing the root causes of conflict and providing people with the resources and support needed to build a stable and peaceful society.

LEGACY OF LEADERSHIP

It's so clear why so many Ivorians believe that Didier Drogba is more than just a soccer player. He's not just a player who scored amazing goals; he's a national hero in Ivory Coast and a symbol of hope and unity. He's a beacon of what the country can achieve when united. Drogba used his popularity as a soccer player to make real changes happen in his country. His actions off the field have made him a true leader and a role model. People look up to him because he's shown that you can use your talent to make a real difference in the world. He's a reminder that no matter where you come from, you can rise above challenges and inspire others to follow suit.

Didier Drogba's contributions to soccer and his efforts to promote peace have definitely been noticed. He has been the recipient of numerous awards and accolades, including the prestigious UEFA President's Award, which celebrates outstanding achievements and exemplary personal qualities. His recognition extends beyond the sports world, with organizations from around the globe acknowledging his work. These awards are not just symbols of his hard work and dedication, but also of the positive impact he has had on countless lives. They celebrate his excellence on the field and his unwavering commitment to using his influence for good, reinforcing his status as a global leader and role model.

Drogba's influence extends to the younger kids, and his legacy in promoting peace through sports continues to inspire young athletes. His story teaches that success isn't just about personal glory but also about lifting others up. Young players look at Drogba and see someone who didn't just achieve greatness but used it to help his country. His work with the Didier Drogba Foundation, which focuses on education and healthcare, shows that sports can be a powerful tool for positive change. Drogba's legacy is a reminder that you can make a big impact on the world with talent and determination. His story encourages young athletes to dream big and use their platform to make a difference. Drogba's actions have transcended sports, turning him into a national hero and a symbol of hope and unity for Côte d'Ivoire.

Activity: Being a Peacemaker Like Didier Drogba

Didier Drogba showed how one person can make a big difference by bringing people together and standing up for peace. Think about a time when you helped solve a problem or stopped an argument. Maybe you helped friends get along, stood up for someone who needed help or found a way to make everyone feel included. How did it feel to do that?

Write about this moment in your journal. Think about what it means to be a peacemaker. How can you help people get along better at school, at home, or in your neighborhood? What little things can you do to make sure everyone feels safe and respected?

Drogba's story teaches us that being kind and brave can make a huge difference. You don't have to be a soccer star to bring people together—you can do it by being a good friend, listening to others, and standing up for what's right. How can you follow Drogba's example and help make the world a happier and more peaceful place?

Hamm

CHAPTER SEVEN
MIA HAMM: A GIRL'S STRUGGLE IN A BOY'S WORLD

"I am a member of a team, and I rely on the team, I defer to it and sacrifice for it, because the team, not the individual, is the ultimate champion."

MIA HAMM

Imagine a young girl in a dusty soccer field in the middle of a small town, where the sun is shining, and kids are running around, kicking a ball with all their might. The girl's ponytail bounces as she races towards the ball. There's something cool about going on here. She isn't playing with other girls. Nope. She's right in the thick of it, competing against boys. Back then, there weren't many girls' teams, so if she wanted to play, she had to join the boys. And boy, did she hold her own! Let's talk about the inspiring story of Mia Hamm.

Playing with boys wasn't just a simple decision for Mia; she had to do it. There were few options for girls to play soccer in the 1980s. The local leagues and teams were mostly boys, and the idea of a girl playing soccer at their level was almost unheard of. But Mia wasn't one to back down. She loved the game too much to let something like team availability stop her. So, she tied her shoes and jumped right in. At first, the boys didn't know what to think about her. Some were unsure, thinking she wouldn't be able to keep up. But Mia quickly proved them wrong with her speed, skill, and fierce determination.

Skepticism wasn't just from the boys on the field. Even parents and coaches had their doubts. They wondered if it was appropriate or even safe for a girl to play in such a competitive setting. This was a time when girls weren't seen as athletic, and seeing a girl excel in a traditionally male-dominated sport was a big change. Mia faced comments like, "Are you sure you can handle this?" and "Maybe you should try a different sport." But instead of getting discouraged, Mia used these doubts as fuel. She trained harder, played smarter, and showed everyone that she belonged. Her parents, recognizing her passion, stood by her side, encouraging her to keep playing and proving the doubters wrong.

Despite the skepticism, Mia's early success was absolute. She had a natural talent for the game that couldn't be ignored. Her performances on the field began to speak for themselves. She outpaced boys older and bigger than her, weaving through defenses quickly and scoring goals that left everyone speechless. These early achievements didn't just earn her respect; they also started to change people's minds. Coaches began to see her potential, and teammates started to appreciate her skills. Mia gained recognition and respect from peers and adults by consistently beating expectations.

As Mia continued to excel, her confidence grew. Each game, each goal, and each victory added to her sense of self-belief. She learned to trust her abilities and to stand tall in the face of challenges. Playing with boys, who were often bigger, taught her to be resilient and tough. It wasn't just about physical strength; it was about mental fortitude. Mia developed a fearless attitude, knowing that she could compete with the best, regardless of her gender. This confidence wasn't just limited to soccer; it spilled over into other areas of her life, shaping her into a determined and self-assured individual.

Mia Hamm's journey from playing with boys to becoming one of the greatest soccer players in history is a testament to the power of determination and self-belief. Her early challenges and successes laid the foundation for a career inspiring millions. So, whenever you face a tough situation, think of Mia and remember that you can achieve incredible things with the right mindset.

SUPPORTIVE FAMILY ENVIRONMENT

One of the most inspiring aspects of Mia Hamm's journey to soccer stardom is the sacrifice and dedication of her family. Her parents, Bill and Stephanie Hamm, played a huge role in encouraging her dreams. Bill, a military pilot, and Stephanie, a devoted mother, balanced their responsibilities while making sure Mia never missed a practice or a game. They saw Mia's passion and talent and went above and beyond to support her. Whether it was driving her to far away matches or cheering from the sidelines, they were always there, her strongest supporters. Their belief in her potential, even when others doubted her, instilled in Mia the confidence to pursue her dreams.

Mia wasn't the only athlete in the family. Her older brother, Garrett, was a significant influence on her. Garrett was like a mentor and a best friend rolled into one. They spent countless hours playing soccer together, pushing each other to improve. Garrett's encouragement was a big motivator for Mia. He would challenge her with drills, race her to the ball, and celebrate her successes as if they were his own. Whenever Mia felt down or doubted herself, Garrett lifted her spirits. He showed her that hard work and perseverance could overcome any obstacle. His influence was a big part of why Mia developed such a strong work ethic and fierce determination.

Balancing soccer with school was no easy feat, but Mia's family made sure she had the support she needed. Imagine juggling homework, tests, and soccer practice every day. It could have been overwhelming, but her parents were masters at helping her find that balance. They set up schedules, helped with homework, and made sure she did well in her studies. They believed education was as important as soccer and wanted Mia to excel in both. Their support ensured that soccer didn't come at the expense of her academics. This balance taught Mia valuable time management skills. It showed her that she could achieve anything she set her mind to with the right support.

Emotional support was another crucial element of Mia's family environment. There were times when the pressure of being a young girl competing in a boys' world got to her. She faced tough days, injuries, and moments of doubt. During those times, Mia's family was her rock. They were always ready with comforting words, hugs, or pep talk. Her parents and brother provided a safe space where she could express her fears and frustrations without judgment. This emotional support was vital in helping Mia stay resilient and focused on her goals. It reminded her that she wasn't alone in her journey and that she had a team behind her, cheering her on every step of the way.

DEVELOPMENT AS A NATIONAL PLAYER

Imagine being just 15 years old and getting a call to join the U.S. national soccer team. Sounds like a dream, right? Well, for Mia

Hamm, this dream became a reality. At an age when most kids are thinking about high school, Mia was donning the red, white, and blue jersey of the United States, ready to take on the world. Her selection to the national team was a testament to her incredible talent and hard work. Mia's early experiences with the team were both thrilling and nerve-wracking. She was the youngest player, surrounded by seasoned athletes, but she didn't let that intimidate her. Instead, she soaked every bit of knowledge and experience like a sponge, eager to prove herself against other countries.

Moving on to her college years, Mia attended the University of North Carolina (UNC), a powerhouse in women's soccer. Playing for the Tar Heels, Mia's talent truly shone. At UNC, she led her team to four NCAA championships. Let that sink in—four championships! Her achievements were nothing short of remarkable. She scored a mind-blowing 103 goals and provided 72 assists during her college career. These stats weren't just numbers; they were proof of her dominance on the field. Her success at UNC wasn't just about the trophies and accolades but about the lessons she learned, the friendships she built, and the confidence she gained. College soccer shaped her into a well-rounded player, ready to take on the world.

Mia's international career was filled with key moments defining her as one of the greatest players ever. One of the most memorable was the 1999 FIFA Women's World Cup in the United States. The final match against China was a nail-biter, ending in a penalty shootout. Mia didn't score the winning penalty, but her leadership and performance throughout the tournament were vital. The image of Brandi Chastain celebrating the winning penalty is iconic. Still, Mia's relentless drive and teamwork helped get them there. Another significant moment was the 1996 Atlanta Olympics, where women's soccer was introduced for the first time. Mia led the U.S. team to a gold medal, scoring crucial goals along the way. These moments weren't just victories; they were milestones that showcased Mia's contributions to the team's success.

Throughout her career, Mia received numerous awards and recognition for her performances. She was named the U.S. Soccer Female Athlete of the Year five times, a record that still stands. She won the FIFA World Player of the Year award in 2001 and 2002. These awards were a testament to her skill, dedication, and impact on the game. But beyond the trophies and titles, her humility and grace truly set Mia apart. She never played for the accolades; she played for the love of the game and the joy of representing her country. Her recognition wasn't just about her brilliance but also her ability to lift her team and inspire those around her.

Mia Hamm's development as a national player is a story of talent, hard work, and a determined passion for soccer. Mia's journey is inspirational, from being the youngest player on the national team to dominating college soccer and achieving international success. Her early experiences, collegiate achievements, key moments in international competitions, and the recognition she received all contributed to her legacy as one of the greatest soccer players of all time. Mia showed that you can overcome any challenge and achieve greatness with dedication and a love for the game.

LEADERSHIP AND TEAM SUCCESS

Mia Hamm was not just a phenomenal player; she was a natural leader, both on and off the field. Leadership isn't just about giving commands; it's about inspiring others to be their best. Mia had this incredible ability to lift her teammates' spirits, especially when the stakes were high. She led by example, showing up early for practice, staying late, and giving 110% in every game. Her determination and work ethic were infectious. Teammates looked up to her not just because of her skills but because she was always there to support and encourage them. She wasn't loud or bossy; her quiet confidence and unwavering dedication spoke volumes. Mia's leadership style was all about mutual respect and leading by example, making her an anchor for the team.

Fostering a strong team spirit and unity was another one of Mia's superpowers. Imagine being part of a team where everyone feels valued and connected. That's what Mia created. She was the glue that held the team together. Whether it was organizing team dinners, leading warm-up drills, or just lending an ear when a teammate needed to talk, Mia made sure everyone felt included and important. She understood that a strong team wasn't just about having talented players; it was about building trust and camaraderie. On the field, this unity translated into seamless teamwork and an almost telepathic understanding between players. Off the field, it meant building friendships that lasted a lifetime. Mia's approach to team dynamics was centered on creating a family-like atmosphere, where every player knew they had each other's backs.

Her leadership was instrumental in achieving major victories, including World Cups and Olympic gold medals. Take the 1999 Women's World Cup, for example. The pressure was immense, with the final match being held in front of a record-breaking crowd at the Rose Bowl. Mia's calm and composed presence helped steady the team's nerves. Throughout the tournament, her consistent performances and strategic plays were crucial. Another standout moment was the 2004 Athens Olympics. Mia led the U.S. team to gold, scoring key goals and providing invaluable assists. Her ability to perform under pressure and her knack for rallying the team during critical moments were pivotal in these victories. Mia's leadership wasn't just about her actions; it was about inspiring her teammates to rise to the occasion and perform at their best.

Mentoring younger players was something Mia took very seriously. She remembered what it felt like to be the youngest player on the national team, so she made it a point to support and guide the newcomers. She'd often take young players under her wing, offering tips, sharing experiences, and providing encouragement. Mia's mentorship wasn't just about improving their soccer skills; it was about helping them navigate the pressures of being a professional athlete. She'd share her own stories of struggles and triumphs, making sure they knew they weren't alone. Mia's approach was nurturing and empowering, helping younger players build their confidence and find their place in the team. She believed in lifting others up, and her mentorship created a culture of mutual support and growth within the team.

Mia Hamm's qualities as a leader, her ability to foster team unity, her role in major victories, and her dedication to mentoring younger players made her an indispensable part of the U.S. women's national team. Her leadership style, characterized by respect, hard work, and genuine care for her teammates, left a lasting impact on everyone around her.

Sawa

CHAPTER EIGHT
HOMARE SAWA – PERSEVERANCE AND LEADERSHIP

"It's easy for people to want to see results quickly, but it takes time. I'd encourage them to keep at it."

HOMARE SAWA

Picture a young girl in a country where women's soccer wasn't given much attention, determined to make her mark. This was Homare Sawa's reality growing up in Japan, dreaming of playing on the world's biggest stages. It was like being a tiny fish in a vast ocean, yet she was still determined to keep swimming.

Homare Sawa was born in Fuchū, Tokyo, a place where soccer fields were more likely to be filled with boys than girls. Though not wealthy, her family made up for their lack of resources with abundant love and support for her passion. Sawa's parents recognized her talent and did everything they could to nurture it. They spent weekends driving her to matches and practices, sacrificing their time and energy to ensure she could play. Their unwavering belief in her was like a warm blanket on a cold night, providing comfort and motivation.

Despite her family's support, Sawa faced numerous challenges. During her childhood, women's soccer was not popular in Japan. There were few chances for girls to play, and those who did often faced criticism and lack of support. Imagine being the only girl in a sea of boys, constantly having to prove that you belong. That was Sawa's reality. She often played with boys because there weren't enough girls' teams. This wasn't just a physical challenge but also an emotional one. She had to deal with teasing and skepticism from boys who questioned her abilities. Yet, every time she stepped onto the field, she played with fierce determination, showing that she could compete with the best of them.

Sawa's early experiences with soccer were a mix of excitement and challenge. Playing with boys made her become tougher, faster, and smarter. She learned to play the rough-and-tumble nature of the games, using her skills to outplay her opponents. These formative experiences molded her into a resilient player, unafraid of any challenge. It was like being thrown into the deep end of the pool and learning to swim through sheer willpower. Sawa's tenacity and skill quickly earned her respect, proving she was a force to be reckoned with. Each game was a stepping stone, building her confidence and honing her abilities.

Her talent was noticed. At a young age, Sawa was called up to the national team, a remarkable achievement that showcased her dedication and skill. Imagine being a teenager and suddenly playing alongside the best players in your country. It was both thrilling and nerve-wracking. Sawa embraced the opportunity with open arms, eager to learn and grow. She trained tirelessly, absorbing every bit of knowledge like a sponge. Her early call-up to the national team was a testament to her hard work and potential. It was like being handed the keys to a treasure chest filled with opportunities.

AT HOME AND ACROSS THE WORLD

Homare Sawa's rise in the world of soccer didn't stop with her early national team call-up. She continued to make great progress in the Japanese league, known as the L. League. Imagine playing in a league where every game is a chance to prove yourself, not just to your country but to the world. Sawa took this opportunity and ran with it. Her time in the L. League was marked by incredible achievements. She scored goals, created plays, and led her team with incredible skill. Each match was a new milestone, and her performances quickly became the stuff of legends. Fans would rush to the stadiums to watch her play, and she became a household name in Japan. Her success in the Japanese league wasn't just about personal glory; it was about paving the way for future generations of female soccer players in Japan.

But Sawa's ambitions stretched beyond Japan. She wanted to test her skills on the world stage, and what better place to do that than in the United States? Playing in the U.S. was a whole new ballgame. It was like stepping into a different world filled with new challenges and opportunities. The competition was fierce, and the style of play was different from what she was used to. But Sawa embraced the challenge with open arms. She joined various teams in the Women's United Soccer Association (WUSA) and later the Women's Professional Soccer (WPS) league. These experiences were crucial in shaping her into a more versatile and well-rounded player. The fast-paced, physical style of play in the U.S. pushed her to adapt and improve in ways she hadn't imagined. It was like going through a soccer boot camp, and Sawa emerged stronger and more skilled.

One of the most remarkable aspects of Sawa's career was her continuous skill development. Even as she matured as a player, she never stopped honing her abilities. Imagine being at the top of your game and still pushing yourself to get better. That was Sawa. She worked tirelessly on her dribbling, passing, and shooting. She studied her opponents, learning their strengths and weaknesses, and used this knowledge to outsmart them on the field. Her ability to read the game and make split-second decisions was unmatched. Sawa became a key player for every team she joined, whether it was in Japan or the U.S. Her leadership, both on and off the field, earned her the respect of teammates and coaches alike. She wasn't just a player; she was a game-changer.

Of course, playing soccer on the world stage had its challenges. Sawa had to overcome not just the competitive nature of the leagues but also cultural differences. Moving to a new country, adapting to a new lifestyle, and speaking a different language were all hurdles she had to go through. But Sawa tackled these challenges head-on. She immersed herself in the new culture, learned the language, and built strong relationships with her teammates. It wasn't always easy. Sometimes, she would get homesick and frustrated, but Sawa's resilience shone through. Her experiences abroad made her more adaptable and resilient, qualities that would serve her well throughout her career.

Homare Sawa's journey through the domestic leagues and international stints was a testament to her unwavering dedication and love for the game. Each step she took, whether scoring a goal in the L. League or playing in a high-stakes match in the U.S., added to her legacy. She showed that you can achieve greatness with hard work, determination, and a willingness to embrace new challenges.

WORLD CUP TRIUMPH

In 2011, Homare Sawa found herself as captain of Japan's national team during the Women's World Cup, a responsibility she welcomed with all her heart. Imagine leading your country onto the field, knowing that everyone is looking to you for inspiration and guidance. Sawa didn't just play; she led by example. Every game, she was the first to encourage her teammates, the first to dive into a challenge, and the first to celebrate every small victory. Her leadership showed what true dedication and passion looked like. Sawa's energy was spread everywhere, and her teammates fed off her enthusiasm and determination. They weren't just playing for themselves; they were playing for each other and their captain, who deeply believed in them.

During the tournament, Sawa's performance in key matches was spectacular. In the group stages, she consistently delivered, scoring goals and setting up plays that left the audience in awe. But it was in the knockout stages where she truly shone. Picture this: Japan facing off against Germany, the defending champions, in the quarterfinals. The pressure was noticeable. Sawa's leadership and skill were crucial in that match, guiding her team through a brutal 120 minutes and into a penalty shootout, which they won. Then came the semifinals against Sweden, where Sawa's quick thinking and precise passes helped Japan secure a spot in the final. Each of these matches showcased her talent and her ability to perform under immense pressure. She was the rock her team leaned on, and she never wavered.

In the final against the United States, Sawa's brilliance reached new heights. The game was a nail-biter, with both teams giving their all. Sawa was playing against the country that helped her become an international star. Sawa's equalizing goal in extra time was a thing of beauty—a perfectly timed flick that sent the ball into the net and the crowd into a frenzy. It was a goal showcasing her skill, poise, and never-say-die attitude. That goal helped push the match into a penalty shootout, where Japan won. For her outstanding play throughout the tournament, Sawa was awarded both the Golden Ball, given to the best player of the tournament, and the Golden Boot, awarded to the top scorer. Winning these prestigious awards was a testament to her incredible skill and dedication.

The impact of Japan's victory in the 2011 World Cup extended far beyond the soccer field. Just a few months before the tournament, Japan had been devastated by a massive earthquake and tsunami. The nation was in mourning, and spirits were low. But Sawa and her team's victory brought a glimmer of hope and joy to a country needing something to celebrate. It was more than just a win; it was a moment of unity and pride for Japan. People gathered in homes, community centers, and public squares to watch the matches, cheering for their team with all their might. Sawa's performance became a symbol of resilience and strength, mirroring the spirit of the Japanese people as they worked to rebuild their lives. The triumph gave everyone something to smile about, something to rally around. It was a reminder that even in the darkest times, there is always hope. Sawa's leadership and the team's victory became a beacon of light, showing that with perseverance and unity, anything is possible.

A ROLE MODEL FOR JAPAN AND BEYOND

After hanging up her shoes and retiring from professional soccer, Homare Sawa didn't just fade away. Instead, she became one of the strongest advocates for women's soccer in Japan. Imagine someone who has achieved so much and then decides that her next chapter is about giving back and making things better for others. That's Sawa. She transitioned into roles that allowed her to shape the future of the sport. From coaching young talents to mentoring upcoming stars, she poured her experience and wisdom into the next generation. In addition, she took on roles in soccer administration, helping to make decisions to ensure women's soccer in Japan had the support and resources needed to grow. It's like she went from being the star player on the field to the coach directing from the sidelines, always involved and making a difference.

Sawa's influence extends far beyond Japan. She's a role model not just for Japanese girls but for all young players. Many young girls would watch highlights of Sawa's career, dreaming of one day playing with the same skill and passion. Sawa's story is a beacon of hope for all these aspiring athletes. She shows them that it's possible to rise to the top, no matter where you start. Her dedication, hard work, and success are blueprints for those who wish to follow in her footsteps. Sawa's legacy is about more than just what she accomplished on the field; it's about the inspiration she provides to countless young girls who see in her a reflection of their own dreams and potential. This global impact is a testament to the power of her story and the reach of her influence.

Over the years, Sawa has received numerous awards and honors, recognizing her huge contributions to soccer. These awards are like glittering jewels in a crown, each representing a different aspect of her remarkable career. From being named the FIFA Women's World Player of the Year to receiving the Order of the Rising Sun, Gold Rays with Rosette, one of Japan's highest honors, Sawa's trophy cabinet is overflowing. But what makes these awards special isn't just the prestige they carry; it's what they represent. They are a recognition of her talent, hard work, and impact on the sport. Every award is a reminder of the countless hours she spent training, the obstacles she overcame, and the incredible legacy she built. For Sawa, these honors are not just personal achievements but symbols of the progress and recognition women's soccer has gained over the years.

Reflecting on her career, Sawa often shares her thoughts on what it took to reach the heights she did and what she envisions for the future of women's soccer. She talks about the importance of resilience, the need for continuous effort, and the joy of playing the game she loves. Her reflections are filled with wisdom and insights, offering valuable lessons for anyone willing to listen. Sawa's vision for the future is one of growth and equality. She dreams of a world where women's soccer is given the same respect and opportunities as men's soccer, where young girls can aspire to be professional athletes without facing the barriers she did. Her reflections are about paving the way forward, ensuring that the path for future generations is smoother and filled with opportunities.

Homare Sawa's post-retirement work, her role as an inspiring figure for future generations, the numerous awards and honors she has received, and her personal reflections all paint a picture of a woman who has dedicated her life to soccer and continues to do so in every possible way. Her legacy is one of perseverance, leadership, and unwavering commitment to the sport she loves. Through her efforts, she has not only left an unforgettable mark on the field but has also ensured that her impact will be felt for generations to come.

OVERCOMING SETBACKS AND CONTINUING TO WIN

Homare Sawa's career was a series of victories and accolades, but like any great athlete, she faced her fair share of setbacks. One of the hardest parts of her career came when she suffered a significant injury. Imagine being at the top of your game and suddenly finding yourself on the sidelines, unable to play. For Sawa, this was a reality she had to confront. But instead of letting it defeat her, she showed incredible grit and hard work in her recovery. She was in the gym, working tirelessly on her recovery exercises, pushing through the pain fiercely. Her determination was like a beacon of light in a storm, guiding her back to where she belonged—on the soccer field.

Even after her recovery, Sawa didn't just return to the game; she continued to perform at an extremely high level. Maintaining such a high performance despite challenges is no small accomplishment. It's like climbing a mountain, reaching the peak, and then realizing you must keep climbing to stay on top. Sawa welcomed this challenge with her usual grit and passion. She trained harder, focused more, and never let her setbacks define her. Every match she played after her recovery was a testament to her resilience. She didn't just play; she excelled, showing the world that setbacks are merely setups for comebacks. Her ability to maintain high performance inspired her teammates and fans alike, proving that true champions rise above their challenges.

Over the years, Sawa had to adapt and evolve her playing style and strategy to stay competitive. The game of soccer is constantly changing, and staying at the top means being able to change with it. Sawa was a master at this. It's like chess players; they always think about several moves ahead. That was Sawa on the soccer field. She studied her opponents, learned new techniques, and adapted her style to fit the needs of her team. Whether improving her passing accuracy, enhancing her defensive skills, or finding new ways to score, Sawa was always evolving. This adaptability wasn't just about physical skills but also mental agility. She kept her mind sharp, always ready to adjust her tactics and approach. Her ability to adapt and evolve kept her at the pinnacle of the sport, showing that staying competitive means being willing to change and grow.

Sawa often shares her personal reflections on overcoming obstacles and the lessons she has learned. Imagine sitting down with her, hearing her talk about the highs and lows of her career. She speaks about the importance of resilience, the value of hard work, and the power of a positive mindset. For Sawa, every setback was a lesson, every challenge an opportunity to learn and grow. She talks about how she learned to focus on her goals, even when things didn't go as planned. Her reflections are filled with wisdom and insights, offering valuable lessons to anyone willing to listen. Sawa's experiences teach us that obstacles are not the end; they are stepping stones to greater achievements. Her reflections are a reminder that with the right mindset and determination, you can overcome any challenge and continue to excel.

Homare Sawa's story is one of perseverance, resilience, and continuous growth. From recovering from injuries to maintaining high performance and constantly evolving her game, she has shown that true greatness comes from overcoming obstacles and never giving up. As we turn the page to our next chapter, we'll explore the story of another incredible athlete who has inspired millions with their dedication and passion for the game. Stay tuned for more tales of triumph and inspiration!

Mane

CHAPTER NINE
SADIO MANE: A STAR WITH A BIG HEART

"I do not need to display luxury cars, luxury homes, trips, and even planes. I prefer that my people receive a little of what life has given me."

SADIO MANE

Sadio Mane's story begins in a tiny village called Bambali in Senegal, where a soccer ball is made from old socks and string on dusty fields. The sun beats down, and the sounds of laughter and excitement fill the air as Mane and his friends play for hours. They don't have fancy gear or professional training facilities, but they have a shared love for the game and big dreams in their hearts.

Mane's early life in Bambali was very humble. His village was small, with limited resources and opportunities. There were no paved roads, modern luxuries, or state-of-the-art soccer fields. The kids played wherever they could find space—sometimes on the school grounds, other times in open fields. They often played barefoot because soccer shoes were a luxury they couldn't afford. Despite the lack of proper equipment, their passion for the game was boundless. Mane's parents were farmers, and like many in their community, they worked hard to make ends meet. The struggles of daily life were clear, but they never let it drain their spirits.

From a very young age, Mane was drawn to soccer. His mother would tell tales of how he would kick anything looking like a ball — rolled-up socks, grapefruits, or even stones. It was clear to everyone around him that this kid had a special connection with the game. His family, recognizing his passion, supported him wholeheartedly. His father might have been skeptical at first, but his mother always believed her son could achieve any dreams he had. Mane would often sneak out to play soccer when he was supposed to do chores. While this sometimes got him into trouble, it also showed his love for the sport. The community noticed his dedication; soon, everyone was rooting for him.

Mane's dream of becoming a pro soccer player wasn't just a far-fetched fantasy; it was a burning desire that drove him every single day. In a place where there were few opportunities, his determination stood out. Mane would practice endlessly, perfecting his dribbling, shooting, and passing. He idolized soccer legends and would mimic their moves, imagining himself on the world's biggest stages. His friends and family often admired his dedication. While other kids might have given up, Mane only pushed harder. He knew that the odds were against him, but he was ready to fight every obstacle that came his way. This unwavering resolve set him apart from his peers.

As Mane's skills grew, so did the praise he received. It started in his village, where older kids and adults began to notice his talent. They would gather to watch him play, amazed at how effortlessly he could maneuver the ball. It was only a short time before word spread to neighboring areas. Coaches and scouts from nearby towns started showing interest. Mane's performances on the local fields were spectacular. He had this incredible ability to outplay opponents with speed, agility, and creativity. The boy who once played with makeshift balls was now being talked about as the next big thing in Senegalese soccer.

His journey from playing in the dusty fields of Bambali to becoming a recognized talent in the region was proof of his hard work and determination. Mane's story began to inspire others in his community. Young kids who played alongside him started to believe that they, too, could achieve greatness. Mane's early recognition also brought hope and pride to his village. Mane's rise was a collective victory, a symbol of what could be achieved with passion, dedication, and a little support.

CLIMBING THE RANKS

Sadio Mane's first big chance came when he joined the local academy in Senegal. It was here that his talent really started to shine. Mane's play on the field caught the eye of scouts, who were always on the lookout for the next big star. These scouts saw something special in him that others might have missed—the way he moved with the ball, his speed, his determination. They knew he had the potential to go far, and they weren't wrong. Mane was soon moved away from his small village to join the academy, a big step towards his dream of becoming a professional soccer player. The local academy provided more training and better competition, allowing Mane to hone his skills and grow as a player.

Moving to Europe was a huge leap for Mane, both exciting and terrifying. Imagine leaving everything you know behind—your family, friends, and culture—to chase your dream in a foreign land. Mane found himself in France, far from the everyday streets of Bambali, surrounded by a new language and culture. It wasn't just about playing soccer anymore; it was about adapting to a whole new way of life. The food was different, the weather was colder, and the people spoke a language he barely understood. But Mane didn't let these challenges deter him. He threw himself into learning French, making new friends, and adjusting to the European style of play. He faced homesickness and the stress of performing well, but he knew this was his chance to make it big.

The early years of Mane's career in Europe were far from easy. They dealt with personal and money problems. Living in a new country came with its own set of challenges. Mane had to manage his money carefully, often treasuring every euro he had. Sometimes, he missed home terribly, but he kept reminding himself why he was there—to play soccer and make his family proud. Training was tough, and the competition was fierce. He had to prove himself every single day, both on and off the field. But Mane's resilience shone through. He never let setbacks define him. Instead, he used them as stepping stones, pushing himself harder and aiming higher.

Mane's time at clubs like Red Bull Salzburg and Southampton marked the beginning of his rise to stardom. At Red Bull Salzburg, he quickly became known for his explosive speed, incredible dribbling skills, and knack for scoring goals. His performance on the field was electric, drawing attention from bigger clubs across Europe. Mane's ability to change the game in an instant made him a fan favorite. During his time at Salzburg, he helped the team win the Austrian Bundesliga and the Austrian Cup, showcasing his talent on bigger stages and catching the eye of scouts from more famous leagues. This success was a testament to his hard work and determination.

When Mane moved to Southampton, he faced the challenge of proving himself in the English Premier League, one of the toughest leagues in the world. But Mane didn't back down. He welcomed the challenge with the same determination that had driven him from the dusty fields of Bambali to Europe. His performances at Southampton were nothing short of spectacular. He quickly became one of the team's standout players, known for his speed, agility, and goal-scoring ability. One of his most memorable moments was scoring the fastest hat-trick in Premier League history, a record that still stands. Mane's time at Southampton solidified his reputation as a rising star, paving the way for his move to even bigger opportunities.

Mane's journey from a small village in Senegal to becoming a standout player in Europe is a story of resilience, hard work, and unwavering determination. It's about facing challenges head-on, adapting to new environments, and always remembering your dreams. His rise through the ranks at clubs like Red Bull Salzburg and Southampton laid the foundation for his future success, proving that anything is possible with the right mindset and support. Mane's story is a powerful reminder that you can achieve greatness no matter where you start with passion and perseverance.

SUCCESS AT LIVERPOOL

When Sadio Mane joined Liverpool in 2016, it was like adding a turbocharger to an already fast car. His arrival was the beginning of something special. One of the most unforgettable moments was his debut against Arsenal. Mane didn't just score a goal; he zoomed down the pitch, avoiding defenders with the speed and finesse that amazed everyone, including the commentators. His goal celebration instantly became iconic, where he joyfully piggybacked on manager Jürgen Klopp. It was the start of what Mane would bring to Liverpool—a blend of skill, speed, and sheer joy for the game.

Mane's contributions to Liverpool's success were plenty. In the 2018-2019 season, he played a big role in helping Liverpool win the UEFA Champions League. His performance in the final against Tottenham Hotspur was nothing short of heroic. Mane's energy and pushing put immense pressure on the opposition, creating opportunities for his teammates. His role in the first goal, where he won a penalty within the first two minutes, set the tone for the rest of the match. Liverpool were the winners, and Mane's efforts were celebrated by fans and analysts alike. It was a testament to his ability to shine on the biggest stages and deliver when it mattered most.

The following season, Mane continued to amaze. Liverpool, driven by Mane's brilliance, finally clinched the Premier League title in the 2019-2020 season, ending a 30-year wait. Mane's goals, assists, and tireless work rate were crucial in this triumph. One of the standout moments was his performance against Aston Villa, where he scored a late winner, showcasing his knack for clutch moments. Mane's ability to step up in crucial games became a hallmark of his time at Liverpool. Whether it was a last-minute goal or a game-changing assist, he always found a way to make a difference.

Mane's reputation as a hardworking team player is well-deserved. His commitment to the team's success is seen in every match. Mane is known for tracking back to help in defense, pressing opponents relentlessly, and creating scoring chances for his teammates. His work ethic inspires those around him to give their all. Mane's humbleness and willingness to put the team first have made friends with his teammates and fans. He's not just a star player; he's the glue that holds the team together, always ready to sacrifice for the greater good.

The recognition Mane has received for his performances is a testament to his impact. He has been awarded numerous individual awards, including the Premier League Golden Boot in the 2018-2019 season, shared with Mohamed Salah and Pierre-Emerick Aubameyang. Mane's inclusion in the PFA Team of the Year multiple times further underscores his consistency and excellence. In 2019, he was named the African Player of the Year. This award spotlighted his accomplishments on the world stage. Mane's recognition extends beyond individual awards; he has earned the respect and admiration of fans and fellow players.

Reflecting on Mane's time at Liverpool, it's clear that he has left an unforgettable mark on the club. His key moments, contributions to championships, reputation as a team player, and the recognition he has received all paint a picture of a player who represents the spirit of Liverpool. Mane's journey from the dusty fields of Bambali to the bright lights of Anfield is a story of perseverance, dedication, and a relentless pursuit of excellence. His success at Liverpool is a reminder that with hard work and a big heart, anything is possible.

GIVING BACK

Imagine having the power to change people's lives in your hometown, making it better for everyone. That's what Sadio Mane has done. He didn't just rise to fame and forget where he came from; he used his success to give back in incredible ways. One of the most heartwarming things Mane did was pay for a hospital in his hometown of Bambali. This wasn't just any hospital; it was the first of its kind in the area. Before this, people had to travel long distances to get medical care, which was very hard. Thanks to Mane's generosity, the people of Bambali have access to healthcare right at their doorstep. It's hard to overstate what a difference this makes for the community. When you're really sick, nothing is more important than being able to get the medical help you need without having to worry about how you'll get there.

But that's not all. Mane also paid for a new school in Bambali. He knew that education was the key to a brighter future, and he wanted to make sure that the kids in his village had the best possible start in life. This school is more than just a building; it's a place where dreams are encouraged and potential is unlocked. With new classrooms, better buildings, and trained teachers, the children of Bambali now have a learning environment that encourages them to aim high. Mane's investment in education continues beyond the school building. He also gives out scholarships and learning materials, ensuring that lack of money doesn't hold any child back. It's like opening a door to endless possibilities, allowing these kids to dream big just like he did.

Mane's contributions extend beyond healthcare and education. He has been involved in several projects to improve life in his village. For instance, he helped pay for the roads, making travel easier and safer for everyone. Better roads mean that people can travel more efficiently, whether it's to get to school, work, or the market. Mane has also supported the development of clean water plants, ensuring villagers have access to safe drinking water. These projects might seem simple, but they have a huge impact on the daily lives of the people in Bambali. It's about making sure that basic needs are met so the community can thrive and grow.

What's truly amazing is that Mane's support doesn't stop after the initial projects are completed. He continues to be actively involved in his community, constantly looking for ways to help. Whether it's through providing gifts or simply being present, Mane's commitment is unwavering. He often visits Bambali, not just as a celebrity but as a member of the community who genuinely cares. His endless support includes helping local businesses get off the ground, providing sports equipment for young athletes, and organizing community events that bring people together. It's like he's always thinking of new ways to give back and make a difference.

Mane's efforts have created a ripple effect, inspiring others to contribute to their communities as well. He's shown that success isn't just about personal achievements but about lifting others up along the way. His philanthropy has sparked a sense of pride and motivation among the people of Bambali, encouraging them to work together for a better future. Mane's story is a powerful example of how one person's actions can have a lasting impact on an entire community. It's about using your platform, however big or small, to create positive change and make the world a better place.

So, when you think about Sadio Mane, remember he's not just a soccer star. He's a hero who has used his success to bring hope and opportunities to his hometown. His big heart and generous spirit have made a world of difference, proving that true greatness lies in how we help others.

INSPIRATIONAL FIGURE

Sadio Mane's story is like a light in the dark for many aspiring soccer players from poorer backgrounds. As a kid with big dreams, you faced countless obstacles. Mane's journey shows that it's possible to overcome those challenges with determination and hard work. When young players see someone like Mane, who started with so little and achieved so much, it fills them with hope. They realize that their circumstances don't have to define their future. Mane's story is a powerful reminder that you can achieve greatness no matter where you come from. It's about believing in yourself, staying focused, and never giving up, even when the odds are against you.

Mane doesn't just inspire from a distance; he gets involved in mentoring young players personally. He understands the struggles they face because he's been there. Mane often visits youth academies and community soccer programs, sharing his experiences and offering guidance. He talks to young players about the importance of hard work, discipline, and staying humble. Mane's advice isn't just about soccer skills; it's about life skills. He tells kids to stay in school, respect their parents, and be kind to others. His presence and words have a profound impact, motivating young players to keep pushing forward and reach for their dreams.

Mane often reflects on his journey with a sense of gratitude and responsibility. He knows that his success isn't just about his talent; it's about the support he receives from his family, friends, and community. Mane believes in giving back because he understands the importance of helping others. He talks about how his journey has shaped him, teaching him the value of hard work and resilience. Mane's reflections show his good character and humility. He never forgets where he came from and uses his platform to make a positive impact. Mane's journey is a story of triumph, but it's also a story of giving back and making a difference in the lives of others.

Mane's story is a reminder that success isn't just about personal achievements; it's about lifting others up along the way. His journey from a small village in Senegal to global stardom is a testament to what can be achieved with hard work, determination, and a big heart. His involvement in teaching and guidance, global influence, and personal reflections make him an inspirational figure for people everywhere. Mane's journey is a powerful example of how one person's actions can have a lasting impact on the world, proving that true greatness lies in how we help others.

Mane's journey from a small village in Senegal to global stardom is a testament to what can be achieved with hard work, determination, and a big heart.

Maradona

CHAPTER TEN
DIEGO MARADONA: HANDLING MISTAKES AND CONTROVERSY

"You can say a lot of things about me, but you can never say I don't take risks."

DIEGO MARADONA

The stadium is packed, the crowd is roaring, and your heart is pounding. You're playing the biggest soccer game of your life. This isn't just any game; it's the World Cup quarterfinals. You're Diego Maradona, the star player for Argentina, and you're up against England. It's 1986, and the tension on the field is electric. The game is tied, and everyone knows the next goal could decide who moves on and who goes home. Now, let's dive into one of the most controversial moments in soccer history—Maradona's infamous 'Hand of God' goal.

In the minute 51 of the match, the ball was kicked high into the air towards the England goal. Maradona, who was much shorter than the tall English defenders, knew he had to make a quick decision. As the ball was falling down, Maradona leaped into the air. Instead of using his head to hit the ball, he punched it with his left hand into the net. The English players were shocked. They immediately complained, waving their arms and shouting at the referee. But the referee, who didn't have the gift of instant replay like we do today, missed the handball and allowed the goal. Maradona's cheeky punch had turned into a goal, and the stadium erupted in a mix of cheers and boos.

The reactions on the field were nothing short of chaotic. The English players were furious, surrounding the referee and demanding justice. They couldn't believe what they had just witnessed. On the other hand, the Argentine players were ecstatic, celebrating as if they had just won the game, even though there were still 40 minutes to play. The referee and his assistants were caught in the middle, trying to make sense of the clashing words. In the heat of the moment, they decided to let the goal stand, and Maradona's 'Hand of God' became final. The tension was real, and the rest of the game had an even more intense atmosphere.

After the match, Maradona was asked about the controversial goal. In one of the most famous quotes in soccer history, he said it was scored "a little with the head of Maradona and a little with the hand of God." This statement added to the debate about the goal. Maradona explained that he saw an opportunity and took it, even though he knew it wasn't entirely fair. He admitted that it was tricky, but in the heat of the game, he did what he thought was necessary to help his team win. His explanation may not have pleased everyone, but it provided insight into his mindset during that critical moment.

On the field, the emotions were running high. For Maradona and his teammates, the goal was an achievement, a brilliant and daring move that had given them the lead. They celebrated joyfully, knowing they were one step closer to victory. For the English players, however, it was a moment of sheer frustration and disbelief. They felt robbed and betrayed, and their anger was evident in their protests and body language. The contrast in emotions between the two teams was stark, highlighting soccer's intense and often unpredictable nature.

REACTION AND CONTROVERSY

Imagine the chaos on the field right after Maradona's 'Hand of God' goal. The English players were absolutely furious. They felt cheated and couldn't believe what had just happened. Some of them rushed to the referee, waving their arms and shouting, trying to get him to change his decision. On the Argentine side, there was a mix of joy and nervous glances. They knew the goal was controversial, but in the heat of the moment, all they could think about was celebrating. Maradona looked around carefully before joining the celebrations. It was a scene of pure frenzy, with emotions running high on both sides.

Fans watching the game had wildly different views. Argentine fans were overjoyed, cheering for their hero and celebrating the goal that had given their team the lead. They saw it as a clever move, a bit of crafty play that had gone their way. On the other hand, English fans were angry. They felt robbed and betrayed, convinced their team had been unfairly treated. Around the world, soccer fans were also split. Some admired Maradona's quick thinking, while others blamed him for what they saw as obvious cheating. The goal sparked heated arguments in living rooms, pubs, and stadiums everywhere, with people passionately arguing about what had just happened.

The media had a field day with the 'Hand of God' goal. Newspapers and TV stations around the globe spoke about the story a lot. Headlines screamed about the controversy, with some praising Maradona's ingenuity and others denouncing the lack of fair play.

In Argentina, newspapers hailed Maradona as a genius, celebrating his ability to turn the game in their favor. In England, the tone was much different. The press was outraged, calling the goal a travesty and demanding changes to prevent such incidents in the future. Soccer magazines, sports shows, and even regular news programs couldn't get enough of the story. The goal became a sensation, with everyone wanting to weigh in on the debate.

One of the biggest discussions that started from the 'Hand of God' goal was about sportsmanship and fair play. Soccer, like all sports, is built on the idea of competing fairly and respecting the rules. Maradona's goal put these principles in question. Some people argued that what he did was simply part of the game, using whatever means necessary to win. They saw it as a clever tactic that added to the drama and excitement of the sport. Others, however, felt it ruined the essence of fair competition. They believed that allowing such actions to go without punishment set a bad example for young players and ruined the integrity of the game.

This debate spread beyond just the fans and media. Coaches, players, and soccer officials all had their say. Some supported the idea that soccer is a game of wits as much as skill, where bending the rules can sometimes be part of the strategy. Others insisted that fully following the rules was crucial for the sport's credibility. The 'Hand of God' goal became a case study in many talks about sportsmanship, ethics, and the balance between winning at all costs versus playing with honor.

The controversy surrounding the 'Hand of God' goal also led to broader talks about how to make the game better. Many called for better ways to ensure fairness, suggesting changes like introducing more referees or using videos to review important replays. These conversations planted the seeds for future progress in soccer, aiming to make the game more just and transparent.

Maradona's 'Hand of God' goal remains one of the most talked-about moments in soccer history. It encapsulates the drama, emotion, and complexity that make the sport captivating. Whether you see it as a moment of genius or a blatant act of cheating, there's no denying its impact on the game and the conversations it sparked about what it means to play fair.

MARADONA'S TWO-SIDED LEGACY

Alright, let's talk about the other side of Diego Maradona in that legendary match against England in 1986. While the 'Hand of God' goal caused quite a stir, Maradona's second goal in that game is often called the 'Goal of the Century.' Imagine this: Maradona receives the ball on their side of the field, surrounded by English players. What happens next is pure magic. He dribbles past not one, not two, but five defenders, making them look like they were standing still. With incredible speed, agility, and control, Maradona glides across the field, leaving everyone behind. Finally, he gets to the goalkeeper, Peter Shilton, and smoothly slides the ball into the net. The entire stadium explodes with noise. Even the English fans, still upset about the earlier handball, can't help but marvel at the fantastic play they just witnessed.

This game showed the controversy and the skill defining Maradona's career. On one hand, you had the sneaky, cheeky 'Hand of God' goal that left everyone arguing about sportsmanship. On the other hand, the 'Goal of the Century' was a masterclass in soccer, showing Maradona's exceptional talent and genius on the field. It was like seeing two sides of the same coin. The same game that had people arguing about fairness also had them standing in wonder at Maradona's incredible abilities. It was a rollercoaster of emotions, showing how complex Maradona was as a player.

These two goals became defining moments in Maradona's career. They combined everything that made him both a hero and a controversial figure. The 'Hand of God' goal put him on the map as someone who would do whatever it took to win, for better or worse. Meanwhile, the 'Goal of the Century' solidified his status as one of the greatest soccer players ever, someone who could do things with a soccer ball that most people could only dream of. These moments are replayed over and over again, each time reminding us of the highs and lows that come with being a sports legend. They became part of his identity, shaping how people viewed him both on and off the field.

Maradona's legacy is a mixed bag. On one hand, he is celebrated as a genius, a magician with a ball who brought joy and inspiration to millions. Kids around the world watch his highlights, dreaming of one day playing like him. He showed us that you could achieve greatness with skill, creativity, and a bit of flair. On the other side, he is criticized for his controversial actions, like the 'Hand of God,' which left a mark on the sport's integrity. His career teaches that greatness often comes with flaws and shortcomings. Maradona's story is a reminder that heroes are not perfect, and sometimes, their mistakes are as memorable as their triumphs.

Reflecting on Maradona's dual legacy gives us a lot to think about. It shows that people are complex, and heroes can have both incredible strengths and notable weaknesses. Whether you admire him for his skill or question his actions, there's no denying that Maradona's impact on soccer is profound and lasting. He left us with unforgettable moments, both good and bad, that will be talked about for generations. His legacy is a testament to the idea that sport, like life, is full of both challenges and moments of pure brilliance.

STAYING FOCUSED

Dealing with intense media criticism can be like walking through a storm without an umbrella. After the 'Hand of God' incident, Diego Maradona found himself in the center of a media whirlwind. Newspapers, TV shows, and sports commentators couldn't stop talking about it. Every move he made, every word he said, was studied and attacked. Imagine waking up every morning to find your name all over the front page with words questioning your integrity and sportsmanship. For Maradona, this was his reality. The constant wave of negative press could have easily broken his spirit, but he faced it head-on.

Despite the media frenzy, Maradona showed a lot of resilience. He didn't let the criticism drag him down. Instead, he used it as fuel to stay focused on his game. It was like he had a shield protecting him from all the negativity. Instead of hiding from the spotlight, he embraced it, always ready to prove his worth on the field. This ability to stay strong and keep pushing forward, even when the world seemed against him, is what made Maradona such an impressive figure. He knew that his actions on the field would speak louder than any headline, and he was determined to let his skills do the talking.

Maradona's professional success continued despite the controversy. If anything, he thrived under pressure. After the 'Hand of God' incident, he went on to lead Argentina to win the 1986 World Cup, cementing his place as one of the greatest players of all time. His performances continued to dazzle fans and critics alike. He moved to Napoli in Italy, where he achieved immense success, helping the team win their first-ever Serie A titles. Maradona's ability to rise above the controversy and continue to excel in his career is a testament to his talent and determination. He showed that setbacks, no matter how big, could be overcome with hard work and dedication.

Learning from mistakes is an important part of growing as a person and an athlete. Maradona's controversies taught him valuable lessons. He realized the importance of fair play and his actions' impact on his fans and the broader soccer community. While he may not have always made the right choices, each mistake became a learning opportunity. Maradona understood that being a role model came with responsibilities, and he strived to improve both on and off the field. His journey wasn't perfect, but it was real, filled with highs and lows that made him relatable and human.

Maradona's ability to bounce back from setbacks and controversies is a powerful reminder that mistakes don't define us. It's how we respond to them that shapes our character. For young readers, his story offers valuable lessons in resilience, determination, and the importance of learning from our errors. In the face of adversity, Maradona showed that it's possible to rise above and achieve greatness. His legacy is a mix of brilliance and flaws, but it's this complexity that makes him such a fascinating and inspirational figure.

LASTING IMPACT ON SOCCER

Imagine you're watching a soccer game, and suddenly, the referee stops play to review a decision on a screen. This might seem normal now, but it wasn't always this way. The fuss surrounding Maradona's 'Hand of God' goal played a big role in creating the Video Assistant Referee (VAR) system. People realized that human referees, no matter how good, cannot see everything, especially in fast-paced games. The 'Hand of God' showed the need for technology to help referees in the right decisions. It started talks about fairness and justice in the sport, eventually leading to the introduction of VAR. Today, VAR helps ensure that every goal, penalty, and offside decision is as fair as possible, reducing the chances of unfair moments like Maradona's goal.

As soccer evolved, so did its rules to prevent moments similar to the 'Hand of God'. Organizations like FIFA and UEFA introduced changes to improve the fairness of the game. For instance, strict enforcement of handball rules became a focus. Referees received more practice on how to spot and handle such situations. The concept of using video technology gradually became popular. These changes were about making the game more transparent and fair for players and fans alike. Rule changes included clear definitions of handball violations and the introduction of goal-line technology to help with seeing whether the ball had crossed the line. These improvements aimed to reduce errors and ensure that the result of a match was determined by skill and fair play.

Maradona's 'Hand of God' goal remains an important topic in discussions about sports ethics. It serves as a reminder of the importance of fairness and honesty in sports. Coaches, players, and officials often refer to this incident when talking about the need for fair play and respect for the rules. The fuss surrounding the goal teaches valuable lessons about the consequences of bending the rules, even if it leads to short-term wins. It's an example of how one moment can shape the ethical means of an entire sport. Educators and coaches use the 'Hand of God' moment as a powerful teaching tool for young athletes. It's a prime example of why fair play and sportsmanship are essential. By analyzing this incident, kids can learn about the importance of following the rules and respecting their opponents. It's not just about winning; it's about how you play the game. Coaches often teach this lesson in their training sessions, emphasizing that the values learned on the field extend beyond sports and into everyday life. The 'Hand of God' is a cautionary tale, reminding young players that actions have consequences and that maintaining integrity is crucial.

While controversial, Maradona's 'Hand of God' goal has undeniably influenced the world of soccer in profound ways. It led to technological advancements like VAR, inspired rule changes to enhance fairness, and became a key example in discussions about sports ethics. Through this story, we see that the impact of one moment can ripple through time, shaping the future of an entire sport and the values it upholds.

Activity: Your Own 'Hand of God' Moment

Think about a time when you did something you weren't entirely proud of, but it seemed like the right thing to do at the moment. How did you feel afterward? What did you learn from the experience?

Write about it in your journal. Reflect on how you can handle similar situations in the future, striving for fairness and integrity, even when the stakes are high.

Maradona's 'Hand of God' goal is a perfect example of how soccer, like life, is full of complex and sometimes controversial moments. It shows that even the greatest players face difficult decisions and must live with the consequences of their actions. As you read on, think about the lessons you can learn from Maradona's story and how they apply to your own life, both on and off the field.

CONCLUSION

Wow, what a journey we've been on together, right? We've seen so much, from the dusty streets of Brazil with Pelé to the bright lights of the World Cup with Megan Rapinoe. We've met incredible players who've faced massive challenges, fought through adversity, and come out on top. And guess what? Every single one of them started just like you—with a dream, a soccer ball, and the determination to make it happen.

Let's take a quick trip down memory lane. We started with Lionel Messi, who showed us that even the greatest players face hurdles. His story of overcoming growth hormone deficiency reminds us that no obstacle is too big if you've got the heart to fight it. We then moved to Cristiano Ronaldo, who taught us the power of a relentless work ethic.

Pelé dribbled his way from poverty to global fame, proving that dreams can come true no matter where you start. Neymar dazzled us with his individuality and fearless self-expression. Megan Rapinoe showed us the importance of standing up for what's right on and off the field. Didier Drogba became a symbol of unity and hope for a country divided by conflict. Mia Hamm broke barriers

124 CONCLUSION

in a boy's world, leading her team to victory after victory. Homare Sawa's perseverance and leadership inspired an entire nation. Sadio Mane's big heart showed us the true meaning of giving back, and Diego Maradona showed us how to stand firm even when people criticize a goal you score.

Now, what do all these stories have in common? Perseverance, teamwork, leadership, and breaking barriers. These aren't just soccer skills; they're life skills. Whether you're on the pitch or in the classroom, these themes will guide you through any challenge you face.

So, what's the big takeaway here? Simple: You can achieve greatness, too. Every one of these legends started just like you, facing their own unique challenges but never giving up. They worked hard, believed in themselves, and kept pushing forward no matter what. And you can do the same. Whether your dream is to be a soccer star, a scientist, a musician, or anything else, take these lessons to heart. Stay determined, work as a team, lead with courage, and never be afraid to break barriers.

You, dear reader, are the future of soccer. The next Messi, Rapinoe, or Drogba could be you. And it's about more than just becoming a great player. It's about using your success to make a positive impact, just like these legends did. Advocate for fairness, support your teammates, and give back to your community. The world needs more leaders like you, both on and off the field.

Here's my challenge to you: Take the inspiration from these stories and run with it. Lace up your shoes, hit the field, and play with passion. If soccer isn't your thing, apply the lessons you've learned to whatever you're passionate about. Face your challenges head-on, work hard, and always believe in yourself. And remember, greatness isn't just about winning trophies; it's about making a difference.

The purpose of this book is to inspire, educate, and entertain you through the incredible world of soccer. I hope these stories have ignited a spark in your heart and filled you with ambition, determination, and joy. Soccer is more than just a game; it's a way of life that teaches us invaluable lessons we can carry with us forever.

Thank you for joining me on this amazing journey through some of the greatest soccer stories ever told. I'm so grateful to have shared these tales with you, and I hope they leave you feeling inspired and ready to conquer your own dreams. Keep playing, keep dreaming, and most importantly, keep believing in yourself. The world is yours to explore, both on and off the field.

Wishing you all the success and happiness in your endeavors. Now, go out there and make your own legendary story!

REFERENCES

Biography.com. (n.d.). Pelé - Biography, 3x World Cup Champion, Brazilian. Retrieved from https://www.biography.com/athletes/pele

Women's Sports Foundation. (n.d.). Mia Hamm. Retrieved from https://www.womenssportsfoundation.org/athlete/mia-hamm/

The Health Site. (n.d.). Lionel Messi was diagnosed with growth hormone disorder at 11: How Argentina football legend overcame it. Retrieved from https://www.thehealthsite.com/diseases-conditions/lionel-messi-was-diagnosed-with-growth-hormone-disorder-at-11-how-argentina-football-legend-overcame-it-936503/

Refrsports. (n.d.). The legacy of controversy: Maradona's "Hand of God". Retrieved from https://refrsports.com/blog/legacy-of-controversy-maradona-hand-of-god#:~

Planet Football. (n.d.). A forensic analysis of the night Real fans stood to applaud Ronaldinho. Retrieved from https://www.planetfootball.com/nostalgia/a-forensic-analysis-of-ronaldinho-earning-an-ovation-at-real-madrid

Men's XP. (n.d.). Cristiano Ronaldo's workout, fitness routine & diet plan. Retrieved from https://www.mensxp.com/health/celebrity-fitness/94489-cristiano-ronaldo-workout-fitness-routine-diet-plan.html

CNN. (2012, March 8). Japan's Homare Sawa: A sporting icon and a symbol of resilience. Retrieved from https://www.cnn.com/2012/03/08/world/asia/japan-homare-sawa/index.html

Encyclopaedia Britannica. (n.d.). Homare Sawa. Retrieved from https://www.britannica.com/biography/Sawa-Homare

Wikipedia. (n.d.). 2018 Ballon d'Or. Retrieved from https://en.wikipedia.org/wiki/2018_Ballon_d%27Or#:~

FIFA Plus. (n.d.). Megan Rapinoe - FIFA Women's World Cup France 2019. Retrieved from https://www.plus.fifa.com/en/content/megan-rapinoe-golden-boot-award-2019-fifa-womens-world-cup-france/bd4786f6-b9e8-4523-ae05-3dd760504a33

CNN. (2017, November 11). How Didier Drogba and his Ivory Coast teammates helped stop a civil war. Retrieved from https://www.cnn.com/2017/11/11/football/ivory-coast-didier-drogba-stops-civil-war-copa/index.html

Biography.com. (n.d.). Neymar. Retrieved from https://www.biography.com/athletes/neymar

REFERENCES

Biography.com. (n.d.). Lionel Messi. Retrieved from https://www.biography.com/athletes/lionel-messi

Goal. (n.d.). Unreal: The Sadio Mané story. Retrieved from https://www.goal.com/story/unreal-the-sadio-mane-story/index.html

Daily Mail. (n.d.). Sadio Mané transformed his poverty-stricken childhood village with a school, hospital, and football stadium in Senegal. Retrieved from https://www.dailymail.co.uk/news/article-12947467/Sadio-Mane-transformed-poverty-stricken-childhood-village-school-hospital-football-stadium-Senegal-girlfriend.html

Printed in Great Britain
by Amazon